PARALLEL UNIVERSE ME HAS NO SCARS

Written by Matthew Stegman

Acknowledgements

    There are only so many thanks I can give. Everyone and everything that has given me inspiration during times where I decided to write something down, thank you. Whether it was a good or bad experience, it was something that shook me. It was an experience that made me move my idle hands to write. I'd like to thank every beer I chugged down in joy or escape, no matter what was going on I had you there. I want to thank every friend of mine who lent an ear when I needed to wail, unable to hold it in. I appreciate every bit of empathy given to me as a present I felt guilty unwrapping. I want to thank my mother and father for always being there for me, for always telling me they chose me, and for always making sure I was okay. My gratitude is endless and will cover this planet until the day that I die. Everyone who supported me when I needed it, I'll buy you a drink when this is published.

    Anyone reading this who doesn't know me, thanks for deciding to pick it up. Anyone reading this that knows me, will know if they deserve thanks or not. If they are unsure then they probably don't. Regardless, I want nothing but the best for you all.

    I love you, thank you.

Contents

The Last Flamingo.................................. 3
Memory Memory................................. 44
Absolute Absence Romance.................... 77
Parallel Universe Me Has No Scars.......... 126
About the Author............................. 180

Parallel Universe Me Has No Scars

The
Last
Flamingo

Insecurities

I think it's a tapping.
Fingers poking the glass,
on the idea that I'm easily replaceable.
It's starting to hurt.
All the evidence is factual,
dissected,
and staring back at me from the table.
What scary glances I get from all of my familiar faces.
"How fun." is satirically whispered.

"Boy, you've got some real issues."
You've whistled amused,
singing notes in threes and twos.
While the affection is diluted down,
three parts water and two parts proper nouns.
A name,
sounds better depending on who's mouth it comes out.

But I'm not complaining I guess,
at the lack of context.
With evidence present it's not a hard concept,
this has just been a good way to kill time.
I've always been a good way to kill time.
Wasn't I a fun way to kill time?
"No." burrows its way into my ear canal.

Impossible Places

You live so far,
and this isn't where you're known to dwell.
There's no reason for you to be in this neck of the woods.
Unless you've come to set them on fire.

Creature with no real name,
is it your choice to destroy or am I giving you the power?
I'll never know.

Your footsteps spread root rot,
layers of filth,
I can feel it infesting my home.
There's no reason for me to see you in this forest.
Unless you've come to set me on fire.

It Was Always a Mess

This has been the fun game where you have to ask yourself:
"Why did I do anything at all?"
and can't seem to come up with a good answer.

Every choice you've made was an effort,
to feel less disassociated,
to feel more connection.
Trying to be human.

It's been a mess.

Be Happy! You're Home and There's Cake!

At the pity party all the balloons are popped.
Every guest has had just enough to drink,
to where they can't drive home.
Nausea sets in.
The line to the bathroom is so long.
You've had enough.

The spirit of fun was there,
and then all too quickly now gone.
You've gotten dressed up for no one to care.

And now everyone is crying,
all the tears accumulate together on the floor,
it's to your shins.
Looking up you see the banner reads:
"Welcome Home"
in unwelcoming font.
Clashing colorful streamers surround you.

It's suffocating,
and the cake is stale.
Welcome home.

We All Learn From Our Mistakes Eventually

Your inability to face any type of confrontation,
is going to be your undoing.
In a panic,
sew yourself to your significant others.
Needle and thread,
hand in hand.
Still questioning if you love the idea of love,
or if you're just terrified of an end.

It's fine,
try not to think too hard about it.
Eventually you'll take a turn,
and smash yourself into an answer,
even if by coincidence.
Sudden self-awareness usually doesn't come easy,
or without smashing into something.

It'll be fine.

The Last Flamingo

Sunshine flickers on your glasses,
walking through all the pink places.
Under arm companion,
dragging its one stuffed foot.
You've got his neck in your hands.
Small traveler with smaller friends.
Young ambition to embrace what you love,
again and again.

Running in excitement you see their balancing acts,
standing one foot,
the edge of a field planted flying roses.
In awe you hop the fence.

When we approach something we love frantically,
it usually scurries away.
You ran to hold them by the neck like you've known,
and kiss their beaks.
So terrified and misunderstanding your intent,
they flapped their peach pink wings to escape.

Falling to your knees in the empty garden habitat,
calling out to them nearly gone.
Your mother approaches and wraps you in her arms.
Held tightly in sunshine,
tears staining your face,
still open-mouthed calling.
Embraced.

Careful With Your Assumptions

If you think you've got any idea about me,
or anything figured out,
I've fooled you twice.
The third time is coming around soon.

Masks line the walls,
and a new one makes a home for itself every day.
I'm running out of space.

You've stumbled upon me,
and my fake mustache.
I'm never the same thing more than once.
Especially if I'm feeling good.
It never stops.
I swear I've changed a thousand times over.

So when you've made your assumption,
don't let it scare you when different shades of color fall off,
like skins I've shed over time.
It's okay if you're having trouble keeping track.
So am I.

Celebrate All the Wrong Choices

Every day you're given a choice. The one you didn't make is made by one of the alternate versions of 'you' spun out across billions of multiverses. So, don't worry, if you made the wrong choice or at least what subjectively seems like the 'wrong choice' to you, one of you made the right one. Celebrate all the wrong choices. Celebrate all the right ones. Celebrate the fact you did something!

We are given the amazing opportunity to choose every day. Do anything! You are what you do. You don't want to be the version of you that does nothing. Coming home from a long day just to fall into easy stimulation for eight hours. Getting calls you're too terrified or apathetic to answer. You don't want to be the version of you that lets their phone calls ring to voicemail and doesn't check it for days.
You can actively decide to stop your self-defeating habits. A little bit of effort to do something goes a long way. The intent to do something goes further than you'd think. You always have that choice. You always have the choice to do.

Think about every choice that has led to where you are now. This moment is unique only to you.
This moment I am ecstatic for you.

Congratulations!

Vulnerability or Instability? Hello! It's Me!

Lately, eye contact has been almost impossible. Anxiety begins to creep up my spine after a prolonged gaze. It is as if my body understands something I don't, and the fear is manifesting the best way it knows how. The alarm has gone off.
Warning! Get out!
My body always knows better than I do.

This has been incredibly defeating. I am trying to be as vulnerable as possible. I want to experience it all completely.

The defeated child becomes the defeated adult.

I will tell you with my absolute biggest grin that you need to be open. I will tell you with my absolute biggest grin that you are enough.

I'll put my arms around you even if I am terrified.
Even if I think you'll kill me.

I'll try so hard to be vulnerable until I actually am.

You Should Think Twice or Maybe Three Times

Think about what happened for a second. Was it really something to shrug off or were you unable to handle it? Did you push it down until it was normalized? Until it wasn't a big deal? You were just trying to survive.

If you're unsure,
a good way to tell is the reaction people give you.

The face they make when you tell a story. The sympathy that they unknowingly let escape. Pity oozing.

When you meet people who have it together you feel yourself start to come loose a little more. This is a good thing. It helps you see by comparison what may have affected your growth.

I've been able to build more of myself now that I've considered maybe some things were a little more impactful than I thought. I've made a map of trickling down trauma. A web of 'why?'

Once you see something from a different angle, you'll never stop seeing it that way. Even if you try to.

This is usually a good thing.

To Everyone Giving Me My Second Place Medals

Melted silver covers my insides,
but I'm still able to cough out **"Thank you."**
Sitting in second place,
you'd think by now I'd be a werewolf's worst nightmare.

Do you think about all the times you were put on the shelf?
Toy in hand or were you the toy?
Or who held you there?
How's it feel to be this way?
Did you get off or did they?

Your attention given whenever you're bored,
imagine me the pot on the backburner,
full of melted silver.
An effort was made to somewhat care,
thank you for your half-assed empathy.

The Largest Rabbit Hole

I'm not afraid of the ground forming the largest rabbit hole,
opening its mouth to swallow me.
Making my descent,
I'll smile and wave to Alice as I fall by.
Drink the juice and eat the snacks provided.
Laugh as the strange surrounds me.
Laugh as I surround the strange.
I will adapt and become vastly anomalous.

I do not fear anything the earth could do,
only what I could do to myself.

Toxic King

Bow to the king of manipulation.
Kneel to the king of molding all his conversations.

His throne is compiled,
of well-timed laughs and even better timed excuses.
His army full of specially crafted jokes for anyone who opposes him.

Watch as he lights the gas under his kingdom,
gaslighting all his citizens.
Watch as he burns down the walls in anger,
out of spite.

Watch as he laughs at all the destruction,
and all too quickly turns to blame you.

The Aftermath

For a moment I found myself in a blissful limbo.
Physical purgatory. I wasn't really keeping track of time.
Clocks are just trying to measure something that everyone feels subjectively. Hours feel like days to me. If I'm under the right type of influence even months.

But it seemed like I was floating. Like time had finally figured itself out in my head. Days scheduled themselves and I didn't need a calendar. My mood elevated and I was up in the air. Standing up fast, the room began to feel like static. I'm ashamed of how much of that is dependent on someone else. I've been preaching to be my own happiness for years. I'm still trying to be.

The same stories keep circling my tongue,
until someone will listen.
Like vultures.
I've got nothing new to say.

So now I seem to be coming down from the high of the stimulation. Reality wants to set in.
An absence forms from losing all the forced physical affection I was given.

I guess I just missed my face being kissed.
I guess I just miss my face being kissed.
I guess.

Crohn's and Me and Everyone Else's Opinion

Your lethargy is frequently dismissed as imaginary, or if you are in pain, it must not be as overwhelmingly awful as you say. Your stomach is never taken seriously. You do not look sick. You have never looked sick, unless the inflammation has run rampant and you're only a few days away from dying. You think its convenient people choose only to believe what they can see. There must be a visible wound oozing or a hospital bill.

You have been told throughout the years that you are too young to be this tired, too young to know what tired truly is. That you have no reason to be as exhausted as you claim. This never ceases to make you livid. Your teapot head coming to boil, about to whistle. However, you always hold your burning tongue.

You feel mentally taxed and angry. Angry that someone could look at you and offer to measure the energy output of your body, like they're eyeing ingredients in a measuring cup. It always seems easy enough to tell you how exhausted you should be, but you've never liked the idea of your well-being measured as one cup or two. It always seems easy enough for someone not to listen.

Any attempt to reason or argue is met with the strongest rebuttals possible. This is the same reaction when you voice an amount of physical pain experienced. It simply could not be that bad.

You've been known to throw theatrics into a boring conversation. You've been known to be the Bugs Bunny or Wily Coyote, so this must be an exaggeration. This must be you acting out in desperate need for attention. There is no way you feel the way you do. There is no way your entire digestive tract could be on fire and yet you still show up to the party or to work. There is no way you could feel on the verge of collapse almost every day sporting the face that you do. You know that any other forms of expression are not acknowledged, but questioned and proven, despite what you say, as false. As if you have no real idea of how your health currently is. Even if it's *your* fucking health.

The Vibrant Good in Others

I think it comes and goes,
its warmth,
sunshine on skin.
It's feeling connected to everyone in the room.
No doubt in your head that you belong.
I wonder if you feel it swelling.
When a sense of self rises from your core,
spreading through your veins,
and spilling out from your face.
I bet others can see it,
and its bright,
it's blinding.
Because I know I have,
but I've never understood,
how someone can exist with so much good.

I've dug deep into the dirt of my body to find sustainable soil.
I will keep looking for the growth.
I will keep trying to create the seeds.
Until I reach a point of light that blinds me,
that's turns me into a beacon.
Until I feel whole,
and finally,
here.

I'm trying to be more than this vile-made human.

Rocketman

Your ego wants to die,
but isn't that the paradox?
That you want it?
To exclaim you deserve it?
To assume you've earned it?

Let's claim your diamond is shining,
when your coal hasn't been pressured nearly enough.
You could travel from Earth to Mars,
and it wouldn't mean you're ready for anything.
I've met some arrogant astronauts.

When things happen, they happen,
and there's no changing that.
Your conditions determine your evolution,
have they been met?
Is there enough pressure to make it happen?

You Have To Keep Writing an Answer

I can recognize the difference,
between being tired and struggling.

Imagine it's a test you're taking,
and all the questions are constantly changing.
It doesn't matter what we write down,
as long as we continue to write down something.
Leaving a blank is failing.

Impulse to Clean

I've pulled everything out of my closet, boxes I've never really bothered to unpack. Maybe I was expecting to move again. Setting things down one by one, dust filled the room. Pulling keepsakes and memory fragments out my hands took turns tracing them all. My floor flooded in papers and art given to me, as if to be put on display. Notes from friends, birthday cards, old wrapping paper I never used. CD's I bought on impulse at small thrift stores. Invitations that haunt me. Books I wanted to read in the moment, some half read, some worn from being treated poorly. Clothes that I'm afraid to wear now, old shoes that I love, and letters written to myself.

Moving things around, feeling them in my hand, I was deciding if I'd like to keep them. Most of them stung to pick up. Pictures I took or that were taken of me. Dates on the back that were never in my handwriting. A photoset of a wedding, someone dancing, and friends I haven't seen in years.

Spread on my floor I had created a memorial of myself, laid askew on my side surrounded by pieces of the past. Renaissance painting. They talked to me for hours.
I found a tin full of ticket stubs from concerts I've been to. Scenes of road trips. Memories of hotel beds and setting things on fire. Nights of connection. Nights not filled with any focus.

It felt uneasy going through everything. I felt uneasy thinking about the last ten years. Categorizing everyone in my life, where they had been and where they are now. A complete timeline was emptying out from my closet. Feeling older than the Earth, I had to throw most of it away.

Most Things Are Not Worth The Energy You Give

I'm not going to argue,
if you're incapable of understanding.
Things inside my head are just the way they are.
You can lead a horse to water but can't make it swim.
You're repeating yourself,
and an absence is an absence,

You keep interrupting me every time I try to explain,
so why bother?
I'm tired of watching all the same patterns unfold,
in everyone I know.
Haven't you learned by now?
You're going to burn your hands when you touch the stove.

I've turned all my heat off,
it's easier for me to keep track of myself,
when I'm not setting fire,
to everything I touch.

Mending The Infection

I've been gargling *self-growth*,
for the past six months,
like salt water,

to slowly mend the infection.

Even if it's taking time,
I can feel the swelling going down,
the anger leaving.
I'm feeling good for the time being.

Let's see if we can keep this going.

Hiding in Public

Overwhelming tendency,
to avoid people who have their lives together.
Yet at the same time remaining envious.
No polite greetings,
I have nothing to contribute.
Just hiding in public.
I don't want to hear about the mundane.
I am on fire.
Every second I have to diminish myself for someone,
is my death.
It is the flame being put out.
It is a metaphor I used in conversation,
that you didn't understand.

I refuse to feel even less than I already do.

Advice

I've got to tell you, I don't want to be the lesson, or the reason for someone else. I am my own reason and will continue to become more of a reason every day. We should all be striving for more than what we're given or what we are, and if anyone tells you otherwise, if anyone claims you're their reason, they're just trying to rope you into some sort of emotional pyramid scheme. It'll be a waste of time and everyone will come out of it a little more traumatized and with a lot less money than when they went in. What an awful thing to do to yourself and someone else, don't you think?

We are all in a perpetual hell of seeking some sort of pleasure. Our brain receives the peculiar taste of dopamine and off we go making decisions like it's a good idea. All our actions only to seek out hedonism in its finest of forms. Poison can taste sweet too, and just because the momentary high feels nice doesn't mean it's always going to.

So let me tell you, throughout your life you will meet certain people and you'll want to unhinge yourself onto them. You will want to remove every part of yourself to replace with them. Try and ignore all of the temptation to do this. Simply be. Simply let the coexistence happen. Allow yourself to be watered by them and always grow for yourself. The second you empty out for them is the second you've lost. They will have become the reason, and later the lesson. It's up to you how many times you will repeat this process.

I know from experience.

Your Obligation To Say Hello To Me

You make eye contact and feel bad about it.
You manage to whimper out a **"Hello."**
with a look of surprise and panic in your voice.

It's not about timing or placement,
it's about every minor detail,
in the five seconds of unprepared conversation,
I've been able to memorize.

The nervous body language,
and where you decide to glance.
Your body frozen in place,
my name being spoken only to fade into a tense stare.
The pressure on your spine,
like unfamiliar hands motioning you to run.
It's the moment of relief when I look away,
It's the moment of relief when I don't say anything.
You've been given clarity,
in realizing that nothing will come from seeing me.

You were able to escape and you feel great about it.

Intensity

From not understanding intentions,
or to being verbally abused and gaslighted.

Is this an irrational emotional response,
or am I just feeling when I'm not expected to?
How intense am I coming off?

How long are you going to try and belittle me,
and what I feel,
because it's too much for you?

I've Always Had an Eye for What's Bad for Me

What keeps me crawling towards the danger?
Is it that in my apathy no one's had an interesting flavor,
or that in any conversation,
it feels like I'm being forced into doing someone a favor?
Could it be that behind their words all I hear is the same whisper:
"Don't worry, only you know how much of a fraud you are,
Mr. Imposter."

I bet you think it takes dedication to be this uncomfortable.
I bet you think you've got me all unraveled.
But I swear it's the only thing that comes natural.
I've never felt so feral.
This is an incompetence tailored to make you smile.
It's all I've got to offer,
to know when it's going to be bad,
to know when exactly to mouth an echo of your words back,
to step into the surrounding danger and feel nothing.

Nothing at all.

A Type of Beauty

Picture me a sugar battalion,
full attack,
catch me next week on the tonight show with Jimmy Fallon.
Bright eager eyes and egg brain fried.
My ego cooked over easy.
If I throw out your name it wasn't for the attention,
I was just feeling tipsy.
It was for fun,
for the laugh,
it was to see what happens.
I'm bursting at the seams with an ominous anticipation.

My swelling sweet victory intuition,
twisting up my face in most situations.
I've seen the future twice now,
yet I never feel good about winning.
With how terrible I am or how I felt,
I'm feeling great now,
as a half asleep caterpillar cocooned.
Sleepy moths fill the room when I finally come to.
I'm flaunting insect wings,
despite what you've tried to call me,
I'm not trying to be beautiful.
I'd rather be the pain that remains unchanged,
in your mouth when you're unable to say,
"Beautiful."

You Should Say Thank You

Sadism is my second nature.
My first is getting lost in any new addiction,
like whiskey or women or mildly interesting fiction.

My hands have been known to act on their own.
So don't mind me inching closer when I start to feel all alone.
It's habit at this point while I'm staring off into nothing,
to cling,
to feel disgusting.

My vices have names,
either attention or intoxication.
I'll never pass up on any free validation.
You know everything here is in the moment,
a constant vibration.
This experience is a gift,
so please show me a face full of appreciation.

Kindred Spirits

You caught me feeling low again,
patches of black sewn onto my loose fitted cardigan.
I'm wondering what on earth this is,
my body becoming strangers churches.
This siphoning of unholy energy,
is just me fighting for dominance.

Do I remind you,
of a collection you once had?
Something made up of so many pieces,
that you'll never get back?
Is it hard to think of all that loss,
or does it not feel so bad?

We share a hunger that mirrors a house burning down.
A hunger that everyone else can see,
and never goes away.
A fire that consumes even when I'm feeling low.
A fire that moves through my every pore.
A fire that everyone else can see,
and can't look away.

Mundane

Tomorrow I will stand in the same place for hours.
Tomorrow I will be polite and charming.
Tomorrow part of me will rupture with each forced interaction.
Tomorrow will be fixated on escape.

Humans are the ever changing variable,
full of surprises.
So I'm trying not to expect anything.
Who doesn't love a good surprise?
Billions of years of evolution,
have bred this special kind of arrogance.
It's also given me the imperfections in my body.
A body that has tried to kill me.

Yesterday I was carefree intoxicated at the bar,
moving from seat to seat.
Yesterday I was drunk enough to escape.
Yesterday I was drunk enough to say how I really feel,
to explain that I've never understood how anyone wakes up,
and is filled with the desire to be alive.
Yesterday everyone's face twisted into pity,
and then just as fast back to bliss.
I've always been good at turning things into a joke.

However today I feel especially weak.
Today I have tried to find my motivation to move and be alive.
Today I have tried to better myself,
for no one other than myself.
Today I simply tried to be.

Get it So Together
That You Could Never Tell It Fell Apart

Something a lot of people don't realize,
is trauma can be the reason,
but it isn't justification.

You're old enough to recognize behavior,
there's no excuse not to do the puzzle.
No excuse to let yourself be this disheveled.
You have to teach your hands,
to stop hitting yourself in the face with a shovel.

So, let's throw a party,
with wine and confetti,
to celebrate your many concussions.
May they be your last.

You'll Want to Watch This One!

Let me teach you,
through example of what not to do.
I'll throw myself off a building,
and impulsively make the situation worse.
I'm known for my infectious laugh and sadistic smirk.
Teeth barely visible.

If bored I will always reach,
for the closest physical destruction.
My fingertips burn at the thought.
It is a pain I'm known for.
I am the embodiment of impulse.

This has always been a form of longing that never goes away.

Becoming The Anchor

It's taken me a long time to figure out that it's okay,
for me to want to be the source of pain,
and not the recipient.
Smile a hello to a face full of excitement.
I will greet you with,
a body raised anchor.
I know there is a certain type of relief,
in rising from the water.
In suppressing my impulse to touch,
or make decisions in anger.

Hallelujah to the vices,
and all of my friends advices,
that I only half listen too.
Hallelujah to the chain that pulls me out of despair,
only to lower me again,
to make someone's ship steady.
To be the lesson learned when ready.
Gasping in asthmatic panic,
small bubbles make an appearance,
to signal my lungs endurance,
during the decent beneath the surface.

We never truly learn anything the first time around.

No Sugar

How do you have it so together?
I've become coffee black,
no sugar.
Your whole persona screams sweet tea.
Perfect pristine peach.
None of that works for me.

Jittery and uncomfortable,
I've spilled out all over the table.
Yet you're so collected,
untouchable.
A true eye candy spectacle.
A real role model to follow.

But you're a little too uptight for me,
I want to be as unkempt as can be.
I want to spill out as much as possible.
A mess no one can clean up.
Not even you.

The Unattainable Sleep

At times life is only surviving.
Late at night I lay down and I force my head to look up,
seeking the unattainable sleep.
Neck curled tight with tension,
throat itching and hoarse.

I'm thinking about survival.
I'm thinking how hard I could press myself into the wall.
I'm thinking of my body twisting into a shape while
dreaming of that same shape.
I'm trying to get comfy.

And when my body has finally stretched and cracked into an unimaginable shape I will have reached the end.

It's so hard to get comfortable.

Escapism? You? Never!

How often do you use other people to avoid yourself?
Have you been doing it your whole life?
Trying not to catch a glimpse of the mirror as you walk by.
It's why everything has failed.
It's hard to see every choice has been to eat up your time.
Love and people and distraction,
right?

So there's been no real focus.
You've been wasting time.
Coping mechanisms turning into locusts.
It's all been a fantastic self-service.
A special kind of black magic.
Escapism is your own veil of hocus pocus.

Because the most terrifying thing to you,
is admitting you need help.
The most terrifying thing to you,
is what you have and have not felt.
The most terrifying thing to you is yourself.

Instinct

Not showing pain has become an instinct.
I've almost mastered the ability,
of never wincing.
Anything can sting if you let it.
Anything can become a wasp if you let it.

When I can handle the silence in a room without panicking,
or planning my escape,
is when you should be scared.
I will have become unstoppable.
Teeth made of knives,
and tongue of mercury.
Something poison and sharp my mouth will have become.

My evolution,
is just how well I've been able to adapt.
Flinching when you've noticed the change,
is common and to be expected.
I'm an assortment of what has managed to survive.
Poisonous if eaten,
you should act with more caution when you walk by.

Parallel Universe Me Has No Scars

Memory
Memory

I've Only Ever Known One Trick and it Was Beg

Everyone I've sang to,
while drunk and numb,
and with plastered grin,
I want you to know I was in pure bliss,
to be the dog howling at you.
The moon who sang back to me.
The moon drunk and orbiting.
Orbiting me when I've been weak.

You've swelled me,
intoxicated.
Smiling,
I've drank all the world's seas.
Spit out mountains to fill the absence.
An animal selfish,
I've been,
to ask more of you.

Old mutt curled in moonlight,
glass and garbage bed.
My collection of surrounding bones scoff,
at all the new tricks I couldn't learn,
but attempted to.
I know it's alright to be selfish sometimes,
to do the tricks that I've always done.

Like Father Like Son

My father says the antidepressants make him feel stupid.
This is the first I've heard of it,
I didn't know he was taking medication.
I didn't know this was going to be our conversation.

I can recall my father working most of my childhood,
a man who took care of his family,
a man I never fully understood until I was in my mid-twenties.
A man who I could have been a better son too.

He didn't mean he felt stupid for taking them.
He means that his thoughts were finally quiet.
There's no longer a hive inside his mind,
where bees bump into each other,
carrying his thoughts back and forth.
No honey,
only lethargy.
Everything slows down,
and he hated it.
A low hum fills his day instead of,
the full weight of an anvil labeled,
mistakes,
or,
regret.

I'm not sure what to say,
I make a joke about Einstein being depressed.
Saying there's a link to depression and intelligence,
that I appreciate the irony of him saying,
the pills make him feel *stupid*.
Like they are supposed to dumb you down.
He laughs.
It's that type of laugh meant to move the conversation along.

It's the type of laugh where something is only mildly funny.
It's the type of laugh we always exchange.

I've never been extremely close to my father,
and he can feel that.
I often have anxiety attacks when I'm under any influence,
about how much I may have hurt him,
in my inability to connect.
I just hope he knows I'm trying.

Moving across country when I was thirteen,
from Ohio to Florida,
I remember cleaning up the house we were going to live in,
and talking to my father.
I remember him saying,
**"You've talked to me more tonight,
than you have in the past year."**

I still think about that often.
I still feel guilty.

Everything's Been Kind of Fucked

Maybe if I started masturbating with my left hand,
the world would start to make sense.
Maybe in a past life I was a lefty,
or got my right cut off getting caught stealing.
Maybe I was impaled.

At this point anything is worth a try,
to make sense again.
Because all I've done is sleep,
and my dreams are getting strange.

And half of being awake is avoiding hostility,
the other half is giving it,
and somewhere in there,
is just numb.
But you should really assert yourself,
yeah you really should.
Give people a reason to avoid you,
and make sure they see the fumes.

Nothing's going to make sense if you keep doing nothing.

It's Hard To Believe It's All Been a Dream

Sometimes,
reality fades in and out of view.

One second you're falling out of a window,
screaming that you're going to die.
The next,
you're watching your body hit the ground.
No blood,
no sound of impact,
just matter occupying space.
It's all you've ever been.

You see people,
glancing down and back up at you.
Handfuls of them whisper:
"What a bad idea."

This pain is imagined but remembered.
This pain is my morning hangover.
This pain is seeing the future,
and thinking up more bad ideas.

The Human Candle

When you're burning on both ends,
the flames have to meet somewhere.

Imagine my body a wick.
Candle wax dripping eagerly to the floor,
as if longing to escape.
Scent of exhaustion fills the room.

How awful I have been.
How awful I have been to myself.

Cosmic Gravestone

In regard to hope, everything's up in the air at this point, either drifting into the atmosphere never to be seen again or falling fast back to Earth to form the blemish of a crater. Maybe even cause some serious blunt force trauma to the head of some poor fool. Despite that and unfortunately for us, humanity's too busy with their hands in their pockets, or grasping their dicks, or on their overpriced phones to try and attempt to catch anything worthwhile. Everyone's left their catcher's mitt at home while opportunity is falling from the sky. Carpe diem, baby.

We've never been good at being in the right time or place, except for the position of our planet. Just far enough from the sun not to cook us and close enough to make sure we don't end up on the dessert menu. Perfect temperature for Goldilocks to barge in, make herself at home, and take a bite. **"Finally, some delicious fucking food."** Gordon Ramsay whispers somewhere on camera.

Ironically though, we are driven to find some sort of purpose or answer. A drive to find meaning in our existence other than all the enjoyable vices available and the genetic urge to behave like rabbits, having as many children as possible. Regardless of the lack of inherent meaning in anything, we seek one. We're just nervous about dying and trying to cement an answer over it all in effort to find relief.

Well, I've got to tell you it's looking bleak. With all our salvation up in the air we walk firmly with our feet on the ground and heads up our asses. Not really minding at all how we're killing the only thing that's keeping us alive. Let's burn the house down while we're in it! On our cosmic gravestone it will read: **"Selfish but not without potential to have done better. Shot themselves in the foot and died cursing everyone and everything else."** It baffles me how evolution can create something so stupid.

Memory Memory

Do you think you'd still be the same person,
if you weren't touched as a kid?
Would you stop wondering if all you are,
is the product of something that happened or what someone did?

Do you think you'd be less angry,
and not hold everything in?
You've lashed out your entire life.
All alone or at least that's how it felt.
Like you've had to atone.

Would your memory come back?
Maybe you'd be able to hold onto all the things,
everyone else remembers but you can't.
Shaking hands won't hold much of anything.
I've dropped everything I've ever been given.

Would certain names never leave a metallic taste,
when trampling over your tongue?
After a while everything tastes like blood.
It's the fear of warmth,
the fear of touch.

You're remembering a scene of devastation,
bodily destruction,
you've always been sick,
this is diagnosed traumatic infection.

So it's not so strange,
that in the moment off key music plays,
that you stumble away,
that you look visibly in pain.
Self-defense and self-preservation,

Parallel Universe Me Has No Scars

it's all been a haunting,
and a revelation.

You've been wondering why you're a certain way,
watching patterns replay.
Erasing the past has been easy,
but it's not getting you anywhere.
The memory is there.
The memory is in everything,
and everywhere.

A body bruised,
floating in water,
algae clinging to your skin.
"Do you think you'd be the same person?"
Do you think that matters?
I guess it doesn't.

A bruise will fade,
even if it's still tender,
You know how to heal.
You've been doing it your whole life.

It's okay if you have to.

What's the Last Thing You Enjoyed? Was it Really Yours?

Addiction to the unavailable.
I love when things are just out of reach,
begging to be touched.
I have a closet full of skeletons,
that never wanted me,
but they're there.

I'll tell you though,
it must be nice to have all those things,
enough to keep your eyes watering.
I'll tell you though,
my hands are aching.
I can't tell if it's the arthritis developing,
or all the times,
I've fallen on my wrists,
falling for whatever walks by.

You know,
I've always had those kinds of eyes.
Honey gold,
amber and dark.
Senselessly searching and then fixated,
on the closest thing to me,
that couldn't feel further away.
Truly unobtainable.

This is Getting Old

One day I'll return,
or maybe I've been waiting this whole time to emerge.
I keep running into lessons I haven't learned.
Face first,
you know this is my own everlasting thirst,
relentless.
Relentless anxious.

I've been told to hold my breath when I'm starting to panic,
feeling as trapped as the air in my lungs.
My mouth making the sounds of a broken bell being rung.
Gasping for no reason.
No inhaler could fix this feeling.
Too many things ache when I start breathing.

When you've felt abandoned your whole life,
it feels a little worse when people leave.
Like they're taking parts of you,
packed in boxes as they drive away.
You can't help but feel the phantom pain.
You can't help but feel parts of you sitting in the passenger seat.

I've always been a passenger,
lending myself to everyone else.
Relentless anxious.

Paranoia Kept Me From Bleeding Out What Else Can It Do?

With no place to go,
my blood still wants to flee.

Bleeding through my pale yellow skin,
to seek something less poisoned.

It asks my body:
"Is this where I truly belong?"
It is met only with silence.
It is given only frustration.

Leaking through to the surface,
Amethyst and magenta,
it asks to be seen.
It asks to leave me.

Sympathetic,
and weak,
I know this blood is mine,
with how stubborn it chooses to be.

Hospital Bed

I spent four days in the hospital recently. Little colorful bruises decided to fill up the surface of my skin in clusters. Even on my crotch! I was very concerned. I went to the ER early the next day. The looks every nurse gave me when I showed them the bruises were very disheartening. I was honestly freaking out. Mostly because they were on my crotch. What can I say? It was alarming. I must have seemed quite the wreck because when the doctor finally came to see me, he told the nurses to give me some Xanax. Which made my visit a lot more pleasant.

After multiple tests were done, they told me that my blood platelet levels were incredibly low. My levels were around 3,000 and plummeting fast towards 2,000. So, if you don't know, like I didn't know, there is a stable range of where doctors want your platelet levels to be at. The level the doctor usually wants a healthy person to be around 200,000. When you have such a low blood platelet level your body has trouble coagulating the blood. Vessels break and blood rushes to the skin to give it a little more color. The doctor told me that my organs could have filled up with blood blisters and the smallest physical trauma like a sneeze or clumsy fall could have ruptured them all. I would have been one popped cherry! They told me if I had not come in, I would have died. This didn't really rattle me as much as it did everyone else. I just told them all: **"Whether I'm alive or dead I'm still me!"** The nurses didn't appreciate the existential jokes as much as I did.

The whole time I was relaxing and reading books in bed. The memories of every time I was in a hospital came knocking on the door to my room, waltzing into it when I asked them politely to leave. I think that's the trickiest thing about memories. It is so hard to keep track. It's so hard to control what's going to manifest in my head and what's going to fall out. Ever since I was a kid I would go and get shots; I would have handfuls of surgeries to fix my body. I remember months of feeling nauseous because I couldn't stop smelling the hospital.

However, most of the film roll memories in my head are full of holes. There are select ones that I can recall, like living in a house with foster kids or my first day of school and bawling my eyes out. Some things are there if I look hard enough, but a good portion is locked away in storage. A storage that for the life of me I can't find the key to.

It's okay though, eventually as I dig deeper into myself, I will continue to unravel. I think for many people it's extremely necessary to explore themselves and question why they can't remember, or why they have certain behaviors. Why they're angry. The more I write about myself and what I can remember the more I start to piece together. The more I recognize my own patterns.

So now I am out of the hospital still feeling weak. I'll miss all my nurses though. There must be a conspiracy going on where they only hire nurses with amazing asses at that place.

The hospital stay was a nice time to contemplate and catch up on reading. I'm glad I decided to go and not bleed to death in my sleep. I've got so much to figure out and do. I've never been one to care about the past, but the memories aren't going anywhere. I just have to find them.

VHS Tapes

I'm only playing back certain memories,
VHS tapes just for me.
Like when I almost punched a dentist,
because it hurt when he said it wouldn't.
My voice full of blood,
and an inefficient amount of Novocain.

Anger in response to pain,
was something deeper inside of me,
than the drill or the cavity.

Or when my dog was shot in front of me.
Gunpowder following the breeze,
and I didn't understand why.
Whimpering bloody,
as his eyes never left mine,
he was asking me **"Why?"**

And when tapes decide to play I still feel the impact.
I'm in the chair again,
and I feel my gums bleed,
as he drops the drill.
I'm six again,
and I can smell the grass and iron as I'm holding a lifeless body.

It's strange what your mind chooses to remember.

The Fear of Intimacy

It's fitting that my body is afraid,
of something that it wants.
Hairs stand on end,
in an effort to protect me.
Weapon wielded.

It's remembering and responding,
to when I had no control.
Overwhelming,
anxious and unyielding,
It's strange to realize,
I've always been weapon wielding.
Knife in hand even when sleeping.

And I'm terrified of relaxing,
of trying to be kind.
Of letting anything unfamiliar,
consume my time.
To let myself be calm enough,
to drop the knife.

Now I'm light headed dizzy,
in a dark room.
Throat sore from all the gasping.
From answering all you've been asking.
My hands find their way to your neck,
in an attempt,
to make it as sore as mine.

You're as Alone as Everyone Else

Sometimes you're not going to feel close to anyone.
There's just yourself!
And sometimes when you do feel close,
it's only because of your memories.
A version of you that no longer exists,
and the person they used to be.
Nostalgia?
Actual connection?
Sugar dissolving in your coffee.

There will be moments where everything lines up.
A bar graph of emotions.
Where it all makes sense and you understand it.
The sun doesn't burn at all.
It's welcoming when most things are not.

When you're someone else's comfort,
favorite pillow or favorite excuse.
When you're waking up frantically searching for a bottle of water, hungover.
Or all the times you felt like you didn't have to look over your shoulder expecting an incoming boulder.
When you've broken down in your friends car,
crying and laughing.
Like it's the first time you've ever felt anything.
It's all been bubbling hysteria,
leaking out.
If nothing else you'd be surprised what we can do on our own.
You can always mend yourself.

A Bright Yellow Sweater You'd Look Great In

I know it looks like I'm standing still.
However over the past two years I've been unwinding.
I've discarded wires,
that have bundled together into layers of knots.
A ball of yellow yarn spun too tightly.
There's enough of me to knit you a decently fashionable sweater.

If you want to see anything correctly you have to learn to separate.
Divide and conquer.
You have to rip things out until it makes sense.
I took each wire one by one,
and tried to remember what part of my body they came from.
Foreign even to me,
but still here.

Everything has been material.
It's the same for you.
It's all been material that you have to mold yourself.
And even if I've been strange,
or deranged.
I'm willing to take the time to do enough to rearrange.
To find closure in closing doors,
and see the ones opening up.
I'm willing to find out how many knots,
and sharp edges are hiding in my body.
Are you?

I've Got to Stop Romanticizing

The closest thing we had to intimacy,
was you crying on my chest about your mother.
And us drunkenly trying to make sense to each other.
I've been a good escape.
Chinese food and wine.
And something in your car died,
when I was in your mouth saying goodbye.

I only remember moments like this,
when I felt something leave,
or when facial expressions changed.
Like when I'm hit in the face,
for opening my mouth the wrong way.
It has more to do with my actions,
than anyone else's reactions.
It's been one big domino effect.
We're all just kids playing with toys,
looking for a way not to feel bored.
The best ways to make nothing into something,
or vice versa.
Romanticizing.

Now I'm lying in a field of weeds,
listening to all the birds complaining and trying to talk to me.
The wind carrying the smell of fire on the last day of
December,
and my reflections of the last year.
Romanticizing.

Parallel Universe Me Has No Scars

I'm Trying so Hard Not to Fall Down

I'm willing to show up to the party,
even if the days been ruined.
I'm the weight thrown around,
during your collapsing exhaustion.
I'm your seemingly never ending energy machine.
Even if bolts are missing I'm still here just for you!
The worst thing to realize is the process lasts forever.
The attempts continue to be attempts,
in the endeavor to feel better.
If you're able to keep staring at the small picture,
with the bigger one right behind it consider me amazed.
Congrats!
Color my small picture green with jealousy.

Anyway, I'll tell you a secret.
If your skin is burning you know you're doing it right.
You have to run like you're being chased.
You have to really want it.
You have to hold the air in your lungs

It's only the second that you stop you should be worried.
It won't happen at first but eventually you'll feel it.
You'll start to notice everything that's got a hold of you.
All the little details leeching on your body will fall off,
lining up dressing themselves as a self-portrait in front of
you.
A mirror image.

And you'll fall down.
You'll fall down and never get back up.

The Egg

I have begun to crack,
yolk and sudden realization running down my face.
Tasting air for the first time I screech.
Retching into a guttural howl as more pieces fall,
I tear at the shell surrounding me.

I have molded hands around my body,
building an egg only I could survive in.
Spiraling back into myself.
Every time I had to grow it was in seclusion.
I had to search for a reason.
I'm looking back at each egg,
at how much filth I had to grow from,
and smiling.

I've figured it out,
that it all has been to repair myself.
When I no longer thought of being alive,
and that this was all just something to leave behind.
When it all felt like endless motions.
It was realigning my feathers,
it was adjusting my beak.
I'm beginning again from the trauma that follows me,
from the misunderstandings.
No more reaching for anything that will have me,
I will reach for myself.
In an attempt to be proud of what I'm building,
in an attempt to become.

I am becoming a person when everyone else already has.

Haunted

I bet the house loves to hear you sing,
so much so it's anxious when you leave.

I could picture it humming,
in the silence fondly,
when it's all alone,
when the walls creak,
waiting for you to come home.

I bet it would catch you off guard,
I bet you'd think it haunted.

The King of Trying to Heal

You look like you'd make a good band-aid.
I could wrap you around all my scrapes and wounds.
Guilt free black and blue,
I'm starting to resemble a bruise.

It's tempting,
but that's not what I'm trying to do,
I'm trying to lead by example.
I'm trying to stop tripping over my own feet,
and let my skin heal on its own.

It's too convenient,
to rely on everyone else,
just to heal myself.

I've always had trouble not picking at scabs.

Red Magnets Red Flags

You can tell me how uninterested you are,
but you're still glancing,
from the floor to back up at me.

The warning in my head has gone off,
but I know I'll ignore it.
Maybe it's all the traits I inherited from my mother.
She couldn't say no to bad things either.

I'm so used to chasing what I should be running away from.
If the danger wasn't there,
my body wouldn't know how to react.
At this point I'm trying to keep track,
of all the things I want that don't want me back.

You don't have to mean half the things you say,
I'm just interested in your devious ways.
Magnets pulling me,
devil hands molding my clay.
You've got me hanging on to every word.

Smother me in casualties until I've become one.

I Fucking Dare You

I dare you to learn something from it.
The constant calling,
the urge swelling up in your belly.

I dare you to force it on to strangers with a smile.
Love bleeding from your gums.

I dare you to care about every person your eyes meet,
to mourn every ghost you walk through.

I dare you to give out handfuls of yourself.
Do you think,
you're able to gift wrap all your problems into lessons?
And decorate your trauma in little bows,
passing them out on the street?

I dare you to try.

Spark the match of your tongue on mine,
convince me it's possible for you to care about anything at all.

Bravado

Bravo to my bravado,
but I'm sick of playing fair.
Showing up bare knuckled,
when everyone's bearing brass.

You'd think I'd start carrying knives,
or find better places to hide.

But part of me thinks I deserve it.

Have you ever failed to hold it together?
Have you ever been a martyr for a cause that didn't matter?

Or one that only mattered to you?

Garbage

Yes you should respect the fact,
that I can throw most things away like garbage.
Yes you should also fear it.
I have no time to remember anything fondly.
My boundaries are two arms in length.

Make sure you've measured the distance,
before attempting to approach me.
Before you attempt to talk to me.

Yes you should respect the fact,
that I can throw most things away,
like garbage.

Bash into Me Like You Mean It

Be the man with the bat.
Be the man with the bat,
that smashes my knee in.

Crushed under the weight,
you could finally be an artist.
Brush in hand,
red paint.

Make as much of a stain as you can.

It's Always Red!

It's gotten to a point,
where I'm not understanding what's in front of me.
What's purposely being shown or what I've accidentally
seen.
No actions line up with the bodies.
No sounds,
nothing is holding its shape.
A language forgotten.

Maybe it's because I haven't had a drink.
All my usual slurs and stutters have no excuse now.
You have to learn how to have a conversation.
No easily accessible exit.
You can't leave the party if it's yours.
You can't end things until they're ready to be ended.

Hues of red hover in the abyss when you close your eyes.
It's always red.
It's always going to be red.

The Boy and His Motorcycle

I still think about the boy and his motorcycle.
I still think about drunk drivers,
whispering to themselves not to fall asleep.
I still think about roadside memorials,
of crying mothers,
and fists clenched in anger.
I still think about the things that keep my friends alive,
and at the same time what's killing them.

And,
I am twenty-five on the verge of a full cycle around the sun.
I am twenty-five years of guilt compiled into an excuse given
lightly despite the seriousness of the situation.
I am twenty-five laying down in the bathtub,
listening to the water drain slowly,
only to be drowned out by my own voice,
as it bounces off the walls in panic.

I still think about the boy and his mother.
I still think about his girlfriend surviving the crash,
inside the ICU.
I still think about it all.

You

You imagine your biological mother playing violin and you're unsure why. You've never met her. The idea of her playing music makes you happy. You're unsure why.

You've renamed yourself the *Problem Solver* because it's easier to fix everyone else rather than focusing on yourself. To focus on yourself means to admit that you need help. To admit that you need help is losing control. When you lose control, you feel like you're dying.

You can't remember what age you were when most terrible things happened to you. You guess. You always say six or seven but you're pretty sure you were younger.
You can't remember anything consistently until high school. Everything else is fragments.

You are afraid. You are afraid only when someone is too close to you. Your hair stands on end like a weapon drawn.

There's something wrong with you but you've ignored it for years. You will continue to ignore it. Ignoring yourself has become a part of who you are. It will continue to be. You've adapted the act of ignoring into being alive.

You can't look at anyone in the face too long. You know they'll expect something human from you. They will announce an emotion you've never felt expecting you to mirror their behavior. You will become increasingly skilled at mirroring behavior as you get older. Learning the reasons behind actions makes you more comfortable performing them. You feel like most things have been a performance.

Parallel Universe Me Has No Scars

You've confused manipulation with actual emotion for years. You have been both on the receiving and giving end of this.

People chewing has become one of your favorite observations. Usually it means someone isn't talking to you.

You often seek the worst possible narrative. This is done subconsciously. This is you seeking what has been familiar. This is you recreating the past.

You still have the knot on the left side of your forehead from running into the tetherball pole in first grade. You held your head in the classroom while drawing. The teacher lifted your hand to see a softball sized knot and called your mother. You had a concussion. No one would let you sleep. This is your only memory of first grade.

You tell people your first experience with death was your dog being shot in front of you. You are unsure if this was the actual first experience or if it was a Siamese kitten dying in your hands after you gave it a bath. You gave it a bath and took it outside. It was winter. It froze to death in your hands. Parts of you still feel guilty even if you were too young to understand why it stopped moving. You've only told a few people about the kitten. It still makes you sad.

You have a hard time connecting to people. You worry that the disconnection is always going to be there. A distant hum that grows louder every day until nothing else remains.

You give up easily. You always have. You hate that about yourself.

Absolute Absence Romance

Parallel Universe Me Has No Scars

Infatuation by Maroon 5 plays in the distance

Infatuation:

noun
'An intense but short-lived passion or admiration for someone or something.'

noun
'Stolen reality. Throwing your body into a river because you think it could win someone over.'

noun
'Love disguised. Absence being filled on impulse. Artificially flavored strawberry candies.'

noun
'Music playing while on a psychedelic. Feels great but will wear off.'

noun
'Feeling empty? Fill yourself with someone else to compensate. Good idea? Of course not, but here you are!'

noun
'Thinking someone is made of ice when you have a fever. Honestly, all you need is some Advil.'

noun
'You're going to be fucking crazy for a while and you won't even know it.'

Parallel Universe Me Has No Scars

THE DEVIL
&
THE HANGED MAN

    One night, like a lot of other nights, I went to a bar with friends. This night I was drinking to reach destruction or relief, whichever decided to appear first. I was drinking to conjure up the blissful numbness as I hit the sheets later that night. Unlike most nights however, a man in this bar struck up a conversation with me. As soon as I sat down, he opened his mouth. I wasn't particularly feeling that great, so I didn't mind the distraction from the night I was having. I ordered a Seven & Seven and he told me he liked me already.

    We talked for the next hour and a half, well he mostly rambled, and I nodded. He told me that he had been drinking all day, making his way from bar to bar. Slurring every other word, he declared that he needed to be drunk to deal with the problems at home. Apparently, he's been married for the last eight years. Swears that he was always loyal and loved his wife. Swears that he was sure she had been cheating on him, that even if he was sure, she denied it. He just wanted her to admit to it. He said he's done everything for her the last eight years, naming multiple opportunities he had passed up on. Exclaiming that if he could, he would have done it differently.

    Showing me the extremely long text message exchange between him and his wife, he grumbles that all she does is attack and instigate when he begs her for the truth. Chugging down my drink, now a Gin & Tonic, I told him that he should see a marriage counselor if he wants to stay with her. While ordering another, I tell him that pain is an incredible teacher and it's going to continue to shape who he is depending on how he reacts to the lesson. That if he refuses to entertain the idea of marriage counseling, if all he can think to do is to sit in regret and drink instead of talk to his wife, and if he has been unhappy with the choices he's made, giving up art and music, giving up his happiness for hers, then he should do them both a favor and leave. Leave and pursue himself and take the time to heal and grow. He didn't like this at all. While calling over the bartender, he told me that I didn't know what I was talking about. That I could never understand. That I listen better than give advice. I laughed and told him maybe he just wasn't very welcoming to constructive criticism.

 Well, I'll never know if his wife cheated on him or if he was stuck in a crazed jealous fueled delusion. Maybe he was just looking for an excuse to leave the life he had, wanting to relive his party days in Germany he kept boasting about. Maybe he just hates drinking alone. Hell, maybe he wanted me to come back to the hotel where he was staying at. He was mentioning how full of regret about his life he was and wishing he could be as free as my gay friends who were locking lips. I'm cute. That could just be my ego though. Who knows?

 Maybe he saw that I was drinking my Seven & Sevens, Gin & Tonics, and cheap beers for the same reasons he was. Not in the literal sense, I haven't been married for eight years. I've been cheated on, but that's not something that matters at this point. Maybe he saw that I too need to drink in my constant state of delusion. It seemed like we were both just used to fanning the fire.

 I'm hoping he goes home and talks to his wife. The optimist in me believes that love conquers all, the pessimist thinks maybe she did cheat on him and I may hear about a domestic dispute in the next couple of weeks if he has one too many Rum & Cokes. If it's all in his head, I hope he can get the number of a counselor and saves his marriage. It's not fair to her either. Staying out all day and night drinking, I'm sure she's worried. All I'm doing is wondering about the life of a man I briefly met, who I will most likely never meet again.

The Devil

Everything plays in reverse,
when you're feeling a certain way.
I've felt tied to too many things outside of me,
my body's trying to keep up.
Feeling restricted,
and bound to my desires.
How do I seem to you?
Hedonistic or satanic?
Maybe just a little odd.

Made entirely of nasty things,
is what you've got in you as vile,
as what I have in me?
Let's get them together and see what happens.

It's never fun playing alone.

Beer and Coffee

If you were to kiss me now,
I'd taste like beer and coffee.
Feels like I've just been drinking to get closer to you.
Do you like that?
Has it been an issue?
Chasing my drinks?
Chasing my own tail in front of you?

Awake but still dreaming,
inside the caffeinated drunken bliss.

What we'd do next wouldn't wake us up exactly.

Alcoholic Neuropathy

My mouth is numb.
I'm starting to wonder,
if I'll be able to feel anything now.

You should touch me,
just to make sure.

I keep drinking to see an answer,
but the answer eludes me.
Is this a surrender into myself?
Or is this an escape?

Can you mouth the answer to me?
I'm having trouble hearing.

The Hanged Man

Who hung you upside down like that?
You look vulnerable and bored.
Stagnant and eager to move.

It's alright.
Even if they're scared,
everyone wants to jump off the bridge,
into a heart filled ocean.
To feel their body break on impact,
as someone else touches them.

The shock to your system makes it worth it.
The static covered fingers grazing on you like a field of cattle.
It's perfect.
You're trying to drown in someone but all you do is doggy paddle.
It hurts doesn't it?

How do you think the cows feel?

You want to divide on a cellular level.
You want all your emotions to bubble up and fizzle.
You want everything to stop moving so fast,
hoping your stomach will find relief and finally settle.

Just try and remember this isn't it,
it's temptation.
You've had more than just your head split.
Your whole body is fighting about who or what to love.

Taking time isn't selfish,
your hearts as soft as shellfish.
Try loving yourself first!
Dumbass.

Dionaea Muscipula

I followed a scent,
sweet.
I came across you,
disguised as a flower.

You hold me like a flytrap,
your drooling jaws felt good as they began to overlap.
The fluids you secrete make my knees wobble weak.

I need to lie down.

Poison in The Bowl

It's not uncommon,
for my best intentions to ruin the party.

Wave hello to the choices I've made,
that have me feeling even more terrible than the previous day.
What's worse?
The one-sided attraction or the lack of attention?
Or spiteful affection?

Sorry,
I didn't mean to poison the punch bowl.

Over Easy

I feel scrambled,
someone's got their hands on my shell.
Slowly applying pressure.
Do they know all my insides are eggs?

You've turned on this heat,
I'm feverish in the frying pan.
Breakfast doesn't usually panic,
does it?
Because I am.

You're cooking me with your eyes.
You're cooking me without even meaning to.

Hurry and take me off the stove before I burn.

Feeling the Opposite of Fantastic

It's mostly pessimism,
why I can't focus.
What a time to be inconvenienced.
Do you think,
I have the time,
to imagine myself in a thousand scenarios today?
Do you think,
I have the money to take a couple shots of distraction?

I don't have anything but cynicism,
no emotions,
no ambitions,
no money,
a bag made of flesh holding nothing.

Where'd You Go?

Have you ever considered letting go?
Allowing your fingers slip from holding the rope?
Imagining a person and then becoming that person?
On every level possible.

You can be more than what you do.
This could be the first attempt at overcoming yourself.

This isn't a way to live.
Being alive could be more than just projection.
Don't you think?

Or have you completely lost yourself,
just because you think you have?

Caught in disconnection.

Funny Games

The thing is,
so many games exist that we could play.
Scrabble?
I could spell out the exact meaning of love for you.
Or steal all of the triple word spaces.
Just to be an ass.
Connect four?
I could always let you win,
because I'm awful at planning,
and it's so hard for me to focus on two things at once.
Operation?
I've had enough surgeries for two people.
Maybe three depending on if the third is a small child.
I'd be an expert,
but you'd have to hold the tweezers.
My hands shake.

But instead,
we play the game of each other's feelings getting hurt.
I'm an expert at that too.
In hurting someone else.

I'm even better at hurting myself without you playing.
Do me a favor and keep score for me.
Do me a favor and write down my score for me.
Do me a favor.

Stop playing.

Parallel Universe Me Has No Scars

THE FOOL
&
THE MOON

    One day at work while extremely hungover, I was cashiering. Frontline of the store, the first one you see and last one before you leave. I was ready to tell you all about the deals and savings. Usually sarcastically, so we could both laugh at corporate America. It was slower than usual, and I felt my knees trying to give in. I must have looked like a building on a construction site, about to fall over.

    I had been working for maybe four hours, not much retail traffic at all, I probably cashed out a total of ten people in that time. I can't stand staying still, my body always feels like it has to keep up with everyone else around me. Like I have to keep moving or I was going to sink into the ground. The tile tarpit had its unrelenting grip on me. The day was dragging, and I felt myself melting into the cash register. Feeling more like a mess than usual, I was unshaven, and my hair looked like a wild animal that had just gotten out of bed. I'm not really one to care about how I look. Ask anyone, I parade myself around all the time, looking less than presentable. The next customer that came through my lane however, made me wish I at least shaved.

    Trying to recall details is hard, it was a while ago, but from what I can remember she was cute. Wearing a black floral dress, she was tall and slender. Light green eyes that she probably knew pierced into anyone she looked at. I was sure I was being stabbed.

    Well, I'm not going to tell you I asked for her number or hit on her. I hate hitting on people. I won't tell you that astonishingly somehow, she fell madly in love with me with little to no contact we had with each other. No one is that lucky. Also, the idea is kind of gross, don't you think?

She came through my lane holding one of those little shopping baskets. Dumbfounded by her, I suppose I didn't fully grasp how many items she had in this basket. I usually do, as I try to bag everything efficiently. I blame that on the nagging desire of being a perfectionist, or is that OCD? Maybe I've just played too much Tetris. When I took the basket from her, I pulled it a bit too hard, my hands expecting a great deal of resistance. No, she must have had maybe five small things in it. I managed to smack myself in the face with the basket. Yeah, I know, I'm smooth as butter, aren't I? Not only did I smack myself in the face with the basket, I also knocked out both the lenses to my glasses. Amazing! I felt like the clumsiest person in the world, as I frantically put the basket down and put both lenses back in.

She was laughing, but it wasn't so bad, I was too. Her cheeks freckled, mine red as the shirt I was wearing. I wasn't too embarrassed, I laughed and asked her if we could pretend that didn't happen. I asked her if we could just pretend that I said something funny. So funny that we both had to laugh. She nodded. I scanned her items and took her money. I gave her the speech about all the deals and cards she could apply for, ironically of course. About to walk away, she told me to watch out, it had been more dangerous than she expected in this store.

I felt silly. I felt ridiculous standing there losing touch with reality because of someone else. There's been a lot of times where my senses were dulled by a pretty face.

Am I Your Pinocchio?

Want me when you want me,
because I'm tired of playing this game.
Threads wrapped around my hands.
From where I am it looks like I'm losing.
Not touching anything.
Tell me more about your intentions.
Tell me more about how you're bored.

The strings you're pulling to make me move this way,
how'd you get ahold of them?
Couldn't you make me move a little close?
As opposed to further away.

Everything could be euphoria.

The Fool

I'm trying to imagine how I look to you.
When I laugh do you see my chipped tooth?
Do you think I have more than one screw loose?
I can picture my face and my stupid grin.
How I move about with no shame,
wearing all my defensive wily mannerisms.

Do you find them appealing?
You're looking at me with big expectant eyes.
It's giving me a certain kind of feeling.

I'm waiting,
for you to notice.
Questioning everything you say,
what's your motive?

Give me an idea of how I look to you?
Probably like an idiot.

They'll Soon Die

I wonder what it is that clicks in my brain,
that makes me feel this specific way.
A laugh or a smile.
Sudden interest or disgust.

A sense of humor is usually a must,
or maybe hair that's dark or the color of rust.

But even if my moths mingle with your butterflies,
even if they manage to fit perfectly intertwined,
a funny thing about mine,

is that they'll soon die.

Even if it's short lived,
whatever made its way from my brain to my stomach,
I'll be sure to feel it.

It'll Be Too Much to Hold In

I want to be so full of love,
that when the doctor cuts me open,
Valentine's candy hearts flood the floor up to the knee.
Doc really won't be able to figure out what's wrong now!

Each one will have a personalized message on it.
There will be enough for everyone in the world.

My blood has been replaced with sugar flavored chalk.

Help yourself.

Stir Crazy

What's made the fish in my head stop swimming?
Is the water too cold?
or has it spotted something it likes outside my fishbowl?

How silly,
that none of my thoughts are kept very good company.
How silly,
that this fish is so lazy.

Golden eyes,
staring out eager,
for something.

Something.

The Moon

An aspect,
barely visible,
not wanting the attention.
Saying you're not even worth a mention.

You're as twisted up as my insides.
I'm going to be tangled for the rest of my life.
In the web we can ignore all the flies,
we can curl up together like a spider does when it dies.

You can't blame me if I see the same thing in you,
howling.

Out of reach.
It's instinct at this point,
I can smell it on you.

It's Embarrassingly Noticeable

It's not my fault all the right lights flash on in my brain,
when you talk to me.
Blinking sporadically,
Fireworks and light shows are filled with envy.
I don't think you're a fan of either.

I'm not sure where to put my hands.
Red means stop and green means go.
But you're giving off a distinct hue of yellow.
Do you know how exhausting it is to do everything in
caution?

Can you see the lights through my eyes?
Or are you even looking?
My spinning disco ball of a head must look so silly.
Especially since no one else is dancing,
except me.

Dancing in Headlights I Mistook for The Moon

Lunacy and idiocy,
have I again,
made someone my moon?
Silly me.
Have I again,
danced on the shores of a beach,
asking the waves to take me?
Whispering quietly **"What's wrong with me?"**

I've spent too much time in wonder,
figuring out again the lessons of my blunders.
The night sky has nothing to offer me,
but I will stare.

I will always stare.

Van Gogh

Van Gogh cut off his ear,
in a fit of rage or panic,
and gifted it to a prostitute.
Maybe he thought she would sleep with him out of pity.
Maybe he was just short on cash.
Maybe he loved her.
Maybe it was just infatuation,
and he took it a little too far?

I could cut off my hands and gift them to you.
Not in a panic,
or so you will sleep with me.
But because the only thing I can do is write.
Isn't it fitting,
I give my only purpose to someone else?
Every time.

THE LOVERS
&
THE MAGICIAN

  Too many times I've weaved a story together in my mind. Trying to make some sort of magic appear in front of me. Usually it leaves me standing confused trying to make someone levitate and they just won't! Imagining things grander than they ever were. You could assume that ant hill mountains take up most of my time. Every day a new one pops up.

  Under the influence of infatuation I tend to turn someone into something they're not. I'm pretty sure I've narrowed it down though, we constantly project what we want onto others. Every day you build up your own narrative for people in your lives. It's an easy spell to cast. I feel as if at certain points of vulnerability, we will do this more than the normal amount and to an unhealthy degree. This is also to say if someone is intense, or takes things to the extreme, they'll give more meaning to the meaningless.

  I'm guilty of losing touch with reality and reading too far into situations. I'm guilty of seeking the lovers. I have painted women, in my vulnerability, as more than what they were. I demanded interactions mean more than they did. It was nothing but magic tricks on my end. The visual of what I lack in myself. I had set up mirrors to see what I wanted. Confusing my reflection projection for them. We are all magicians seeking the magic. Seeing things through roses.

  The illusion or our subjective fantasy of the lovers is what keeps us going in the attempts to be touched. Desire to validate our own existence with external means, rather than internal. Which usually never works out. Try not to get confused.

Do They Sell Whatever You've Got?

How are you so vibrant?
Does the Sun fall asleep at your command?
The Moon and Stars must visit Earth to see you.

You're smiling with emotion,
with something,
with love so easily.
I can't figure it out.
I don't understand.

Don't mind me casting glances.

The Magician

I'm not made to last,
I just want to love while I'm here.

But who am I to say anything,
about the only real magic left in the world.
When I've barely scratched the surface.
I want to dig in with both hands,
without shaking or feeling nervous.

All I am is me,
I'm still ecstatic,
eczema skin elastic.
A real physical affection fanatic,
unable to truly function without it.
With my heart screaming on my sleeve,
I must really seem quite dramatic.

Don't you ever get tired of acting that tough?
I'd rather be inviting,
or enticing.
To be able to have enough,
to where I feel warm to the touch,
fresh out of the oven,
a real cream puff.
Aren't you curious about the magic?
Are you open enough to love?

Delusion Left Unchecked

The ability to turn any situation,
or thought into physical matter.
Manipulated by voices I've made up,
a mocking bird's made it's nest in my head.
Who said what exactly?

My ears burn when I hear anyone talk,
if it's not about something they want.

I've molded what is into what isn't.
Picture me coiled,
a snake biting its own tail.
This is my perpetual cycle,
of delusion.

I'm often caught guilty of creating what shouldn't be.

The Lovers

You could be the end of me,
natural enemy.
Perfect predator.
The wasp to my bee.
Not that I have anything worthwhile,
just honey.

But you know lover,
I'm sitting here with nothing to offer.
I don't have what it takes to play,
in the animal kingdom today.

So go ahead and eat me.

Better Lock it Next Time

I'm pretty good at opening Pandora's box,
and even better at putting everything back in it.

I gave you a good scare, didn't I?

Don't worry,
not even all the chaos in the world,
is too much for me to handle.
Just hand me the lid,
and pretend nothing happened.

Pretend I never happened.

Hand Holding

You cannot create or destroy energy.
That emotion you felt has always been there.
The energy used to lift your hand to their face.
It's always been in existence.
It wasn't created,
or when they left,
destroyed.

Allow yourself to remember,
that everything you've felt or will feel was already there.
Just waiting for the magic,
for you,
or someone else to wake it up.

We always have that energy there,
it may just be a little surprising when we finally notice.

Houdini's Denial

You're starting to know when you're making a mistake.
The key is reacting and pulling off the sheet,
of your bad habit magic tricks.
You can't keep making everything disappear Houdini.
Naivety up your sleeves,
you've made all your choices vanish into thin air.

There is no accountability for you.
There is no remorse.
Are you an addict to starting over?

"Abracadabra"

DEATH
&
THE TOWER

I've spent so much time ignoring the banana peel, slipping and falling. I felt it was time I finally picked it up. I'm nothing if not someone who learns from experience. After falling head over heels and busting my ass over a few pretty faces, I've found myself in a good state of mind. **"Hello sanity, nice to see you again. It's been too long."**

You can ask anyone I know, if you ever meet them, that I am a strong advocate for transformation. Just don't ask for any embarrassing stories! Maybe you'll hear about a couple of my breakdowns. There's plenty to fill another book. On shelves near you soon: *The Big Book of Matt Needs Therapy*.

Anyway, what are you doing staying the same for so long? The whole point is to further ourselves! In any way possible. I need to feel a constant flow going upwards. Infatuation is a big eye opener of what needs to change. Oh boy, did you really spend so long pining for someone? Someone who never saw the reality you created. Did you give them a personality tailored for you? When you could have been bettering yourself? It's okay though, you learned a good lesson, didn't you? Sorry to say, but if you didn't, you'll be repeating a lot of the same mistakes.

Let's do our best to get to stability! Get to a place where someone is no longer the priority. The priority is you! Well, for me, it's me, but you get the idea. I've had to push and discipline myself to stability that is not external but internal. My stability is me and I will continue to build more of it. You should too.

Hello Siren,

I can taste the salt on your lips.
It stings like a warning given too late.
Bad intentions creep up from behind you.
It's intoxicating,
the feeling of suffocating.
I swear you've got your mind set on killing me.
Gasping for air,
I can't see the surface anymore.

I don't remember leaving my reason for being on the beach.
But it sounds like something I'd do.
Absent minded,
I've often been that kind of fool.

**"Don't fall in love with mermaids,
they just want to drown you."**
I should have listened when they warned me.

I'll know for next time.
What a good lesson this will be.

To Become Even More

Pain helps us survive.
It tells us what not to do.
It helps us know when to run.
I've met a lot of people who,
can't stand the idea of being hurt.
Don't you want to learn?
How you work?
What works?
What you need?

If I have to experience the end,
over and over again.
That's fine.
What doesn't kill me just gives me more reason to exist.
I'll get it right eventually.
Let me learn through trial and error.

Let me be vulnerable and open.
Exposed wound in sunlight.
Healing.

The Tower

I will kiss my mistakes on the cheek,
and say farewell.
Pushing my naivety out of the nest.
Things feel never ending when you never move.
I've seen the same view from atop the tower,
for the last couple of years.
A new perspective from falling off,
is what I've needed.

Can you stay the same for so long,
that your body becomes a statue?
Do you still retain any virtues?
With a body of stone,
can you still move?

I step one foot off in a gamble,
telling myself it's something only gravity can handle.
The wind feels nice,
as I watch the sky grow farther away.

I've spent too long with my head in the clouds.

Coy Koi

I've been dropping my love into your fountain,
wishing for you to come out of the water.
I figured I'm worth more than a quarter.

Maybe you don't find it appealing,
even if at the bottom it's gleaming.
Specks of red cover the surface,
as I ask you to come up.

You'd think I made the fountain my alter,
with how much of me I've offered.
When it's all just been to feel,
to feel something a little softer.

But it's alright if you're doing just fine,
I can find other things to take up my time.
Don't worry,
anything I've given to anyone,
is theirs to keep,
including goodbyes.

Too Easy to Fall Into

I appreciate,
how you've kept my foot off the gas pedal of my insecurities.
Silk to the touch,
I've been wrapping myself in you.
Expecting the warmth I feel to keep me company.

I fear I have given too much of myself away,
to try and hold onto your hand.
I fear you have given away too much of yourself,
to offer your hand.

I need to reel myself back to reality.

Death

A person exists somewhere inside of me,
holding onto all of my empathy.
I rarely see him,
he's always on his way.
Whispering something about dying.

Maybe he's afraid to let me hold it.
Maybe he's afraid I'll be clumsy and break it.
I never see him long enough to ask.

Secluded somewhere,
always in a hurry.
I figured there was no point in running from death.

But you know,
some parts of us know better than we do.

What Goes on in My Brain When Threatened with a Seemingly Stable Relationship

1. "Oh my God, what are you thinking?"

2. "I am frequently caught up in my own delusions of grandeur while at the exact same time feeling like I'm not enough"

3. "You must have awful taste."

4. "What trauma or self-destructive behavior led you here?"

5. "I will dismiss the last few years of my life sooner than relive them."

6. "Eventually you'll see I am a wound wrapped in a band-aid of jokes and the skill to always deflect. No substance."

7. "I won't be able to touch you without wincing."

8. "You won't be able to touch me without wincing."

9. "I tend to never let go of control. Being in a relationship would be the opposite."

10. "I refuse to become a part of something again."

11. "What the fuck am I supposed to get you for your birthday? I'm terrible at gifts."

12. "No one here is obligated to endure or deserves the inevitable panic that I will bestow upon them."

How Strange

You called me strange and I liked it.
You said I had to be insane and I liked it.
I told you there are plenty of people like me,
you just haven't met any yet.

"Where are they hiding? Cause you're all alone."
Is what you told me.

I couldn't help but agree with you there.
It's sad but I still liked it.

How strange.

What is the Modern Romance?

Tom Robbins seemed to think the modern romance revolved around redheads, homemade bombs, and a pack of Camel Cigarettes. One could claim that he had a craving for the eccentric. Seeking spectacular life changing acts of expression only rivaled by a nice piece of ass or an even nicer piece of philosophy. Robbins would have you teaching a monkey how to steal a diamond or how to hitchhike without holding out your thumb. All for the sake of the experience, he'd tell you to eat a mushroom and go looking for dragons to slay and princesses to save, while teaching the exact opposite as a lesson. **"We are our own dragons as well as our own princesses. You should focus on saving yourself from yourself. Although, you should definitely keep eating the mushrooms."** Defying society's laws and making up his own, he would persuade you to believe that all of this is the modern romance. That nothing truly surpasses the natural passion of a well-timed introduction, good conversation, and a bottle of tequila. Maybe a little bit of anarchy if you're feeling frisky. The cocktail you'd drink before leading to orgasm.

Shakespeare would argue that the modern romance is filled with dramatic poses, overwhelming hysteria, and daggers held by our lovers. **"Oh, what bliss could this love lead me to? Alas, this winding road may make me weary, I shall see my sweetheart if the end is nearing."** When really it was a trail of breadcrumbs naive lovers followed spiraling down into a descent of madness. Often the romance shared in the world he saw, ended in tragedy. **"If not a death**

by the hands of a beautiful woman, did my life matter at all? Was it truly worth it to live without her love?" What Shakespeare wanted to convey truly was the flaws of romance. What can and will go wrong while the lovers quarrel? The mistakes and repercussions of good intentions. Will someone get mauled? Will an entire family be thrown into despair and chaos for one's own political gain? Sex, betrayal, drama, and poison. The sir and madam of the house greet you kindly, grit their teeth, and put on a show asking you to come into their lovely home. Stabbing each other to death later that evening, with or without you present. You've been to some awkward dinners before, but this one certainly makes the top five.

    Sam Pink, through various metaphors and strangely descriptive tales, will try to show you that the modern romance is lying face down on the bathroom floor, avoiding puddles on the ground in fear of what could crawl out of them, and imagining a stranger holding you in the middle of the night brushing your hair while you sleep. How much of yourself can you ignore by using someone while at the same time how much of everyone else can you ignore by isolating yourself? He will tell you that you're worthless on your own, and that your survival is dependent on as many people you can use and hurt. Modern romance is no romance at all, simply trying to sustain yourself is enough. Breaking down what it means to be a person inside of a person and how to hurt both. **"Yes, I can use this. Yes, I can use you. You can be my pillow when I have nothing left. I will be what you run to when you have nothing left."** If you could sneak into someone's house and hold their hand at night, is that not

Parallel Universe Me Has No Scars

romantic? Even if it's only romantic to you? Even if you're the only one that knows. Sam urges you to try. He may know no one can do worse to him than he can, but he should probably work on being a little nicer to himself. The modern romance being that there is no romance, just using one another. Organisms in a mutualistic relationship, but as humans, we are destined to make sure it ends badly. We are the puddle and what crawls out of it.

    Matthew Stegman one day while pondering on endlessly, concluded that the modern romance could resemble something as simple as a gas station rose and a four pack of Pabst Blue Ribbon. That it doesn't have to be overwhelming stimulation, or grand gestures that parade around the details of one's bank account. That a few beers, a gift, and rough sex that leaves both involved in a state of euphoria mixed with asthma could be enough. If you find him, either coffee or beer in hand, he will offer you a funny story, an unwanted book recommendation, and an unyielding ear that listens to whatever you'd like to talk about. You must listen to him ramble in return, which if he sees opportunity to, he will strike. He asks that you trace over everyone's actions twice to find the true meaning behind them, even if you must make it up on the spot with little evidence and speculation. He would tell you that the highest form of intimacy available would be shoving your panties in your mouth. This is followed by a smirk, a wink and a laugh. The Master of Mediocre Advice, The King of Discount Therapy, Matt would tell you that the modern romance is simple and doesn't have to be defined. That the truest forms of romance have always been and always will be simple, but it is us, the ones involved that complicate it. That it could mirror the effort it takes to subdue the fear of being touched or quirky jokes that fly quickly but elegantly over most people's heads. Modern, post-modern, or ancient, he thinks either way you shouldn't take it so seriously. **"Kiss each other and enjoy it, but make sure there's lots of tongue."**

Absolute Absence Romance

Most days nothing too interesting occurs at your job. You clock in and do the same thing you did the day before. Maybe make jokes to your coworkers, then go home. Most days there is nothing too exciting going on. You've seen people trip and fall in the parking lot, seen screaming children be carried out, and seen someone get tackled by security more than once. He isn't really allowed to do that but oh well, he stopped a guy from stealing, give him the award of Not the Best Decision but Things Worked Out. You deserve the same award but for different reasons. You're used to nothing interesting happening, but recently something did.

After selling someone something they didn't need, one of your managers walked by putting a walkie away from their mouth and back to their hip. They asked you to keep an eye out for someone who had been walking in the store for a little over an hour. She gave a vague description to look for. She asked you to let her know if he was acting strange or looked in distress or angry. Being the Curious George that you are, you ask why. What had this boy done or was suspected of doing?

It turns out another coworker had issued a restraining order on her significant other. You are shocked to think that the guy decided to come into her workplace. You were at the ready to report any suspicious behavior, but alas your watchful eye caught no one fitting the description given. You figured maybe he had risked enough just by coming in and quickly left.

The time came for you to take your break, feeling hungry and tired you walk to the coffee shop in the front of the store. You slept too little the night before, your body needed its caffeine and frozen breakfast sandwich. As you walk up, you see a police officer standing next to a table where a man is sitting, hands behind his back looking up at the officer with a vacant expression on his face. Yes, this must be the man in question. As to why he was sitting in the shop handcuffed and not in the back of the cop car, you'll never know. Walking by, you catch the last bit of their conversation. The officer looking down, asks him why he would come into her job after multiple warnings and the restraining order. A blank veil still on his face, his mouth begins to warp into a smile. **"I don't know. She's the love of my life, man. The love of my life."** He let out as his smile began to crumble back in on itself. He then became vacant again.

Ordering your black coffee and sandwich, standing to the side to wait, you thought hard about this. The love of his life? Could he really say that? You looked at him and wondered what kind of life he could be living to give it's meaning to someone else. A case of infatuation creating delusion to that extent. You think about how many times you had become something similar. Something that would give someone else more meaning than they should have. You had done this. You had given that power away and emptied yourself. Sporting the same vacant stare. How many other people have let this happen to themselves? Turning others into something they were not. Burning for something they made up. The minutes it takes to get your food feels like an eternity in your head.

When your name is called, you snap back into the current moment. Yes, you are on break. Yes, you have no time to waste in this corporate world. Making your way through the door to the breakroom, you turn back to see the officer leading him out of the store. You think of every man who has hurt a woman because of their own delusions. You think of how easy it was for anyone to get lost in their head and come out worse off than before. You walk into the break room and see a woman standing in the corner. You see her on the phone shaking, police officer next to her. Sitting down the opposite end drinking your coffee fast. You look down at your sandwich untouched. Seems you've lost your appetite.

Parallel Universe Me Has No Scars

You Died

You died. Well good job, idiot. We all have one important thing to do and that's self-preservation. You know, keep yourself freaking alive. Drink water, eat healthy, and maybe occasionally exercise. Do your fucking best! But I mean, it was bound to happen at some point so try not to beat yourself up about it. Don't look now but you seem to be materializing in a very dark room. Your eyes are still adjusting, so you can't really make out what's happening. You try to move around, but you can't feel your legs, in fact you can't feel much of anything. Hey, reminds you of being alive doesn't it?

You hear loud humming noises. They're overwhelming, like an ancient air conditioner that's on its last leg. An ancient air conditioner that's letting out a howl to let you know it's dying. You can't really remember dying, so you try to think if you howled or not. Various images of wolves tearing apart your body and howling in unison flash into your mind. Although, you were nowhere near exciting enough in life to be torn apart by wolves.

You hear a voice welcoming you. It's raspy and like the stubborn AC Unit, overwhelming. You're unable to make out a face, and you can't even tell where this voice is coming from. It's all around you, like the echo at the Grand Canyon. Not that you've ever been, but you could imagine.

Great, dead and surrounded by very loud nothing. Loud everything? Maybe God? You never were very religious, and you'd rather had just turned into worm food rather than hear a lecture from an *almighty being*. Let's not get too existential. This probably isn't the best time.

The voice congratulates you on making it as far as you did. Wow, you don't really feel like you did anything congratulations worthy while you were alive, but hey take compliments where you can get them. Way to go! Praise is praise, flattery can get this voice everywhere. The voice begins to ask if you'd like to peer into the lives of different universe versions of yourself before being thrown back into the cycle of energy. Birth and death. You think to yourself that it must be a test. Some kind of *ego measuring*. Like, you're that concerned about different versions of you. Conceit or curiosity? Suddenly, for some reason all you taste is burnt coffee. Terrible. Terrible free burnt coffee you had at an orientation for a job. The secretary was cute, and she really knew how to burn the coffee. Her yellow dress comes to mind and is gone in an instant. What were we talking about?

Anyway, about this multi-dimensional viewing! Well, what the hell right? Might as well get one last show. You doubt any good Netflix originals are going to be at the ready while you're being turned back into energy or whatever is going to happen. For all you know this loud talkative voice has plans to turn you into a cockroach! Not that it wouldn't be a familiar feeling. Damn, you never finished a couple of shows you were watching. Damn. What other strange things could happen in that show? You'll never know now.

You nod. The darkness in the room slowly starts to illuminate. A thought enters your mind at this moment, that maybe this is hell. The voice could have lied to you, hot flames everywhere the second you agree to anything it says. You really should have asked for a contract to read. On the fine print could have been: *Welcome to hell! Where you get to watch every other version of you do the right thing, because all you've ever done are the wrong things! Also, it's really hot!*

You let out a **"Well, fuck."** Before getting slightly dizzy. Light flashes in the center of your vision. Swirling colors fill the room until you can make out a figure that from what you remember, looks tremendously similar to you.

Windchimes Devouring a Midwestern Home

In the summer of 2001, I laid in a field of dandelions.
Staring into the distance,
where the sky meets the earth in a gentle embrace.
Surrounded by gold and yellow,
I listened to a symphony played on windchimes.
As if it was only meant to be heard by me.

I was the local hero even if only to myself.
That day's conquered was a hornet's nest.
The beast I fought to prove myself.
None of the kids believed I would do it.
That I would knock it loose from the tree.
They ran as I turned around big grinned.
I was too proud to run.
There were no spoils of war only casualties.
The only casualties being me.
Still smiling,
my face was swollen bright pink and yellow from the stings.
They had their revenge and I felt alive in the land of weeds.
It was amazing how calm I felt,
when I could have been stung to death.
There is no mercy in the hornets kingdom.
Not that I deserved it.

I left the battleground and collapsed onto the welcoming field.
Letting out my victory cry,
I threw my weapons into the air to show the world I had won.
There were no witnesses.
If you asked me to destroy a hornets nest now,
I don't think I could.
There is no victory in meaningless death.
There is no reward,
in taking the life of something just trying to live.

Parallel Universe Me Has No Scars

There are no windchimes where I am now.
Nothing since,
has compared to the stillness and calm,
I felt as a child in that midwestern home.
In that field of weeds and wildflowers.

Calm even if burning,
bruised yellow stings covered my yellow skin.
Nothing has engulfed me like the sound of windchimes on a
windy summer day in the Midwest.
Like the whole world was simply a field of dandelions,
growing just for me.
Not asking a single thing.
Other than to exist,
to learn,
and to listen.

The Unwinnable Battle
and The Last Of My Resistance

How much of my body was made from obligation?
Everyone seems to know me better than I do.
Think they could figure it out for me?
Picture me a Venn diagram,
full of gin and awful insults to myself.
Only ever to myself.

This is a new feeling in my chest,
like I'm trying to vomit the last twenty-four years.
Do you know what it feels like,
for your own body to attack other parts of it?
To try and crawl out of the war?
To never get any rest?
Well I've been nothing but the embodiment of it.

And when I die leave my head unburied,
leave my eyes open,
so I can watch the world come to an end.
You know it's something I've been hoping to be a part of.
If only as an audience.

Knife Fights and Arguments at My Funeral

I've caught myself staring,
it's easy to get lost in the scenery.
It's easy to catch yourself,
feeling greener than the greenery.
Everyone is standing in the funeral of envy,
not a single word is said as the casket lay open.

My body's been cut into squares.
This has been a combination of feeling secluded and separated,
like I've been sent to factories to be sanitized and packaged.

Mail me to my exes doorsteps,
and anyone who I've wronged,
I want them to get the worst parts of me.
So, there's a wave of nostalgia to blanket their face,
when they open the box.
Hide the few better pieces,
from anyone who could get their hands on them.

It's so easy to be spiteful.

Risk Taker

Sometimes you have to take the leap,
skateboard downhill,
or try and challenge gravity,
by jumping off the roof,
and almost die.
You never know,
you may just enjoy where you land.

Alternatively,
you may break both your legs.
But you'll get some sweet ass casts.
Cute girls will want to sign them too!
Well, maybe not,
you jumped off a building you dumb bitch.

No one really understands anything,
until they really get there.
That includes falling.
At least in the world of theater,
you'll be twice as lucky now.

So better start your acting career!

Asphalt Mouth

    I've had my jaw broken and wired shut to fix my underbite, but I've never gotten into accidents so badly that I broke a bone. I've never had a cast. So maybe that's why it's alluring, the jump, the dive into the asphalt mouth. The ache in my bones to experience it just once.

    I spent over two months in Tallahassee, and about a week in, I was skateboarding to grab breakfast with a buddy. I felt so good going down the hills. It had been one of those periods of my life where I wanted to lay down and not get up. Spreading roots into the Florida sand and gasp for nutrition. At least I had my friends to pick me up. Although, we all have to learn to stop reaching to others for sustenance at some point.

    A big part of me wanted to slam into the trees that waited slightly to the left at the bottom of the hill. I wouldn't have to worry about anything anymore and the trees looked like they could use some decoration. I started thinking about my life and where I was. How nothing made sense anymore and I was just riding the waves waiting for something to stick. How I was riding the skateboard downhill not listening to the warnings of my friend. The peripheral view of a car heading my way jolted me back into that moment. I put my foot down ignoring inertia and the speed I was going, flew forward and flipped twice. Hello, gravity.

    An overwhelming wave of defeat smashed into me right as I smashed into the ground. I've always hated losing. The searing pain throughout my arm kept me from yelling back. Thinking back now, I feel as if the trees wouldn't have done as much damage as I thought they would.

    I caught myself on my right hand and left elbow, trying as hard as I could not to slam my face into the concrete. My face is a solid six and a half, I had to keep it that way. Parts of me are left on that road in Tallahassee. Just like parts of me are scattered across the country. My elbow was seared and the skin on the palm of my hand was gone, pink remained and was now oozing blood. Blood coming to the surface as fast as it could to escape my body. Finally, free!

I remember the pain coming and going in unpredictable intervals. Everything slowed down and I was excited. It felt good. It had been so long since I got hurt. I was lucky I didn't break my wrist. I was lucky I didn't get hit by that car. I was already pretty much homeless, and I didn't need that extra stress of a broken wrist or a broken everything that I couldn't afford to see a doctor about.

I stood up and laughed as my friend frantically asked if I was okay. We joked about it the rest of the way to breakfast. I laughed when I bandaged myself in the fast food places bathroom thinking about the blood they were mopping up. I laughed eating my chicken sandwich and fries. We laughed on the walk home. Everything had always been a joke for me. It was the easiest way of dealing with it.

He congratulated me for surviving. I congratulated myself. Tally hills take no prisoners. I felt good. I felt better than I had that entire year. Blood dripping down the bandages onto the concrete, the street's asphalt mouth was satisfied. There was no ache or sting the whole walk back. It only hurt when I tried to sleep, when I didn't have anything to distract the pain. A concept I am very familiar with.

I bet parallel universe me would have nailed it. No fear and no distractions. He would have been able to see the future. He would have fucking nailed it. Skated right past the car without panic and done a sick kickflip. Me? I can't do any tricks, but I bet he could. Proud of his entire life and living for fun, he wouldn't have thought about crashing into the trees. He wouldn't have felt lost in a city with his best friends. He wouldn't have felt lost at all. Everything works out for the version of me that has it together.

He would have been just fine.

Accents

I like to imagine my biological mother,
with a thick Korean accent.
It just makes sense,
that if we met I wouldn't understand her.
That everything she said,
would match my idea of her.
Unfamiliar.

Maybe that's why half of me,
wants my tongue to learn the language.
And the other half spits at the thought,
it's still dripping heat heavily,
steam rising angrily.

Forgiveness is divine but I'm merely me.

Mother but In Korean

I've been reading a lot lately about trauma and how it can be passed down from our parents. I've been reading a lot about how things shape us when we are younger. How parts of our family stay with us long after they are gone.

Anyway, as I read about the inherited trauma and learned more about my biological mother things started to make a lot of sense. I started to see less of the picture I painted of her. I started to empathize more with her as a human instead of demonizing her as someone who abandoned me. That was how I viewed her my whole life, as someone who didn't want me. I never truly tried to think of her experiences or her circumstances.

One day I worked up the courage to ask more about my biological mother. Which I was always stubborn about, exclaiming that I didn't care and that it didn't matter. Another thing that stopped me in the past, I was afraid of hurting my adoptive parents by asking. Something that I found out was that she herself was adopted from Korea. I am unsure of the exact situation, but I was told she had an abusive adoptive father. The more I think about her experiences, the more I can understand exactly why I was given up as a baby. I understand the reasoning of why she was the way she was. Which is so important for any kind of closure. If the person is not there, we do our best to find closure for ourselves.

Being Korean in a place where there are little to no other Koreans present could make you feel like an alien. It's how I have felt in the past. No real connection to heritage or family history. This could explain why I myself have felt disconnected my entire life. Maybe growing up with an abusive father and the inability to connect with her biological parents had affected her relationship with her child and even the idea of having children. Maybe the fact that she was given up as a child made her question herself if she would be able to raise a baby. The only reason I think this now is because I have struggled with the thought of having children. A big voice in my head was always saying: **"You have her blood in you and you'd be unable to love your child."** Which I know now is ridiculous and isn't the case because I am not my mother. I am a completely different person. I am myself and I am able to see now that she was more than just someone who couldn't love her child. She was just a person. The nonexistent relationship she had with her mother affected her relationship with me. Nonexistent.

    I've been able to tie what I know about my mother to more and more of my behavior. I've been able to openly think about the things that have happened to me personally and how they affected me and my relationships. Ever since I started to analyze myself more, I've been able to see patterns in myself and learn how to stop them. It is my responsibility to untangle myself from what happened to her and trickled down to me. It is my responsibility to become better than what I have been previously due to inherited trauma or my own traumatic experiences.

    The information I have is just from what I've been told. There's no factual evidence. I would have to have a conversation with her. Even so, if I only have so many pieces to the story, I am doing a lot of healing. To stop and consider my mother as a person helped me become more empathetic and compassionate. I am noticing how even if my biological mother gave me up for adoption, I am full of her unintendedly left behind traumas. I am full of her blood. I am full of my father's blood who I have not learned one thing about. I am full of reasons to heal.

    It's incredibly important to, if you're able, talk to your parents about their past. To talk to them as another person and not just your parental figure. Try to analyze and figure out what makes them the people they are. Which may be easier for you than it was for me. We grow up thinking our parents have it all figured out that they are complete people, but no one is a complete person. I've had to force myself to have conversations with my adoptive parents about things that sting to talk about. In doing this, I learned more about them and myself. From learning about their past traumas and experiences in their childhood, I could piece their lives together and learn why they are the way they are. Which meant that I could figure out the similarities between them and myself. I have established more of a relationship with both even if I pushed them away as a child because of this. I have been able to see them as both my parents and as fellow humans.

Mirrors

Day one

Another day that starts in front of the mirror. Thinking back, you can't really remember getting out of bed, walking to the bathroom, or stepping in front of it, but hey, we're here aren't we? Better brush your teeth. Show off your polished pearls. Trying to remember walking into the bathroom is like trying to remember a dream after waking up and falling asleep again. Five times. You just can't. Unless you're keeping a dream journal, but what kind of nerd does that? For some reason you do feel as if you had a nightmare though. You vaguely remember being in some sort of panic. Some sort of fear. Maybe if you were one of those nerds, you'd remember why. You laugh to yourself, toothbrush in mouth. Although, everyone has trouble recalling things in the morning, don't they? You're pretty sure you simply don't have full consciousness until about ten minutes after waking up. Who knows what sleepy you does? Pomading your short shaggy black hair back, you think about buying a journal but then quickly dismiss it. Well, it doesn't really matter. You didn't think this hard in the morning yesterday, from what you remember, so what's it matter? Get dressed and make sure your face looks good. You must start the day.

Day two

Okay yes, you hate work, and waking up, everyone does, but you cannot stand in here for twenty minutes looking at your own face cursing the day. You're going to be late and it's just not very productive. You dread the idea of losing another job. The manager at the last place you worked screaming at you flashes into mind and then is gone. Screw that place anyway. Also, did you drink last night? You're not sure. You don't smell like whiskey or gin, your favorite choices, or look like you're hungover. Your head is just feeling groggy, again. Maybe a little worse than yesterday. Looking into the mirror, between your slightly grown out facial hair and the shirt you don't remember buying, you think to yourself it's time for a trim and that you should stop using Amazon Prime for all your shopping. However, you've got to stop hating being in public first. You switch the light off, and out the door you go. Goodbye weekend, hello office job.

Day three

You glance at your reflection for a second before opening the medicine cabinet. Still half asleep you pull out a few bottles, the ridges feel good on your fingertips as you trace them. Somehow it dawned on you this morning that you'd been forgetting to take them. You think to yourself they must be important if they're here. Somehow just slipped your mind. You've always found yourself hesitant on taking medicine, but there must be a reason you have them. With a groan, you take two of each, and splash some faucet water into your mouth with your hand. One painful gulp and it's done. Smacking your cheeks in victory you exclaim **"Took the medicine!"** while throwing your fists in the air. You try to remember if your doctor told you not to drink on these, but his words are fuzzy. In fact, everything is kind of fuzzy. Television static found its way out of the appliance and into your head. Who let that in? Did it sneak in through your ear? Deciding you don't have time to worry about it, you close the cabinet, glance at yourself one last time, and start to leave. Thinking to yourself that this new job must be killing your attention span and short-term memory. It's a lot of typing. Your face seemed a bit off, more than usual, and you don't even recall getting home last night. You made it somehow. You hold yourself in high regards on the ability to always make it somehow. It's one of your few talents. Another is forgetting names within minutes of hearing them.

Parallel Universe Me Has No Scars

Day four

Alright. Pills, check. Shaved face, check. Wallet, watch, and phone? Check. You look at yourself and find the reflection staring back at you annoyed. As it should be, didn't you learn how to shave when you were sixteen? Somewhere around there? You open the cabinet and pull out a small bandage, peeling it and placing it onto your jawline slightly left of your chin. You think to yourself that you can't afford to bleed on everyone as you place another on your neck. Barbara at work will make a comment, you're sure of it. That woman loves to talk. **"Nicked yourself shaving there, huh? You know my husband..."** She would trail on and on. Everyone there seemed to enjoy a conversation that was full of unnecessary details. You think to yourself that life is mostly full of unnecessary details. Oh well, it is what it is. Closing the cabinet, you turn to walk away, but as you do your peripheral catches something odd. It was as if for a second there was a delay in your reflection. Only for a second you saw yourself not moving. Standing still, like someone else was in the room. Odd. You remember reading somewhere about the delay in senses. That your brain kind of cheats at showing you things. Always making things up so it's easier on you. Feeling unnerved. You speed walk into the hallway. Thinking it was nothing. Feeling silly for even being bothered. You're not a child, you don't have time to be afraid of your own reflection. Come on.

Day five

Absolutely ridiculous! Your inner monologue declares. Stepping out of the shower you grab a towel. Another argument won only in your head. You manifested your coworker taking credit for your workload, and instead of nodding and smiling, this time you let him have it! Demanding the credit instead of passively handing it off to the highest bidder. The award for standing up for yourself in your head will be placed on your shelf. Congrats. You hang your head in shame as you dry off your hair. **"I've really got to get it together. My whole life is coming apart."** You mutter to yourself while pulling a shirt over your head. You're not wrong. After doing all the things in your morning routine, you make a mental note to become better at standing up for yourself. You're as good as you think you are. So, start thinking you're great. You look in the mirror and bring an L shape to your forehead and stick your tongue out. A sense of humor is important. After bringing your hand down and grazing your face slightly you wince in pain. You notice an unsightly bulbous mass near your left eye. It's as big as the eraser on a pencil, it makes you immediately think of high school. Poking it again brings you back to wincing. It hurts. It's a pimple. Stress acne. Great. You let out a sigh into your hands and drag them slowly down your face. **"Fuck this job, it's making me break out. I'll pick up something after work."** You grab your phone off the sink countertop and leave. While thinking of looking into other employment opportunities, the left side of your face aches. You can feel your left eye twitch in unison to the pain.

Day six

You feel awful. Reaching your hands up to your head you groan in pain. How did you make it out of bed? You're unsure. Did you beat the shit out of yourself in your sleep? Maybe another nightmare. All you can picture is hands grabbing at you from every direction. Day of the Dead flashes into your mind. It sends shivers down your back as you place your hand on the mirror. As you swallow the medicine you think of a bus deciding to park inside your bedroom, on top of you. The driver getting out and kicking your still sleeping body, then he would have gotten back into the bus and did donuts. At least that's what it feels like. At

Parallel Universe Me Has No Scars

least that's what you imagine had to happen for your body to feel like this. Sweaty with a fever, aches and sore all over, you stare into the mirror. Satirically you offer the glass reflection a wide smile and point at it. **"Way to go champ!"** you spit out with no enthusiasm. The reflection returns the satire with its own. Looking down at your pajamas you pull your phone off the countertop and dial the office. **"No way I'm working like this."** After giving you some speech about being responsible for your own health, you're hung up on. They weren't happy. They'll have to deal, won't they? Fuck this. Go back to bed. You lean on the doorframe feeling your face. It's drenched in sweat and clammy; it even seems as if your acne is getting worse. Maybe it's just the fever but it stings even more than yesterday. **"Feet of mine lead me to my kingdom of pillows and hopefully sweet dreams."** You whisper as you walk away from the bathroom. Sense of humor is important.

Day Seven

Staggering into the bathroom you manage to lift the toilet seat and vomit up whatever you ate last night. You can't remember what it was. Shaking and holding your sides you rest your head on the seat. Gross. Your face feels like it's on fire. It feels like you're allergic to the oxygen in the room and your skin is reacting accordingly to the allergy. **"Shit! Why do I feel so bad?"** You exclaim while pulling yourself up by the edge of the counter. This is the worst you've felt in years. Even worse than that break up last summer when you were dumped. Wait. What was her name? You've been having trouble remembering small things, but this is weird. Breathing heavily, you open the medicine cabinet looking for your pill breakfast. Sweat dripping eagerly off your face you take one bottle out. It slips from your grasp and end up on the floor. **"God dammit."** In frustration you slam the door to the medicine cabinet shut and bend down to pick up the bottle.

They should make these things less slippery. Especially when you feel like shit you think to yourself. Standing back upright you see that you slammed the door so hard you cracked the mirror. Way to go. Immediately after seeing this, you catch the blemishes near your eyes moving as if something is trying to escape. You let out an agony filled wail as it feels like something is trying to emerge through your face. **"Fuck! What the fuck!?"** Holding your face in your hands you apply pressure to the now searing mass as to contain it. You think maybe this is another nightmare. An extremely vivid one. After smacking your cheeks, a couple of times to wake yourself you look up. To your surprise in the cracked mirror you see what looks like another eye coming out of the mass! Alright, dream or no dream this is fucked up. A foreign eye coming out of your cheek and looking around! After it hurriedly darts its gaze, scanning the bathroom, it focuses in on you. Screaming in pain you begin to scratch and dig at the unfamiliar eye. **"Fuck this! There's no way this is real!"** You yell as blood trailing down your hands and arms as you reveal more. The burning becoming more intense and unbearable you see that it isn't just a third eye developing. It's a whole other face! A whole other face is fucking coming out of yours and it doesn't even look like you! You're terrified. You can't feel anything anymore. The pain has subsided and been replaced with an overwhelming fear. You look back at your reflection to see the left side of your face covered in blood as the now red and irritated third eye continues its way through. The fourth now barely visible. You're coming apart! You've been falling apart your whole life and now this is happening! The universe decided you are shit at being alive and is replacing you! Violently! Fuck! Without hesitation you angle the left side of your face towards the mirror and smash it through. Completely shattering the mirror and your now horrifying reflection. Things get hazy as you feel your body become heavy. You start to imagine becoming best friends with whatever is coming out of your face. Ridiculous, but to be fair you've felt lonely lately. Your body hunches over the countertop and falls to the bathroom floor. Dream or no dream you feel your consciousness begins to fade. A faint hum begins to fill your ears that over the next several seconds becomes a high pitch ring. Dream or no dream this has been an awful experience. Everything turns to black.

Day Eight

"God, my head hurts." You say while scratching your head and then pulling off your shirt you walk into the bathroom. You're sure you weren't out drinking; you don't smell like beer or cigarettes. You only smoke when you drink or when you're forced to talk to someone for an extended amount of time. You ignore it. You don't have time to worry about this. You just started this new job and need to leave. Lately, your days and nights have blurred together anyway. Toothbrush in mouth you wink at yourself as you brush little circles over your teeth. Minty fresh. **"Maybe I'm just dehydrated."** You think to yourself. Grabbing your wallet and keys you begin to head out the door. Right as you're about to leave you catch something move in the corner of your eye. Weird. Looking back startled you scan the bathroom, your search ending with your reflection in the mirror. You smile and wink to yourself. **"Let's go"** You whisper as you turn and leave through the door.

Every day the mirror gives us some reassurance when we see ourselves in them. Throughout the day we can only assume that we are still us. There is no evidence until we glance at our own reflection. Yes, that's me. Hello, me. Oh, I should probably clean off that smudge on my cheek. Yes, okay, we look great. Let's go. Do you ever see yourself at the exact moment of dissociation? Do you ever disconnect from your train of thought? Changing tracks so suddenly that you barely notice? Do you ever see someone else in the mirror? Often, I have dissociated while looking in the mirror. One second I am there and the next I am gone. I wonder if one day something else will come and replace me in that millisecond I am looking at myself. The small window of opportunity for something to sneak up from behind and take my place. I've had dreams of crawling into the mirror and everyone speaking backwards. I've hallucinated my face splitting apart more so than how it already has. How do I know it hasn't already happened?

Was That Genuine?
Or Only What Felt Comfortable?

I had to give up the need for control.
Pretend every angle is just the thrift store polaroid.
It's all a show that I've been performing in.
It's a gag and I'm either laughing or,
I'm driven by a divine annoyed,
brandishing a look of disgust.
My face a face to avoid.

All the pictures taken of you,
each one a different person entirely.
A life of misunderstandings,
and every memory,
tightly wrapped in napkins.
You're unsure of how to handle this.

The last five years have been dependent,
on the lightning in the room.
Flickering confusion,
to music slightly out of tune.
You're stagnant but always moving,
phasing between shades of red and blue.
You always see bad news,
drape alluringly like a noose.

And your favorite sport is hiding,
because you're committed to it.
Because you're good at it.
Because you've always hated being in the open.

What Time Is It? Tooth Hurty

I don't know why,
the American Dental Association,
wants to rob me at gunpoint,
for just wanting to smile.

Because my mouth fucking hurts,
and I've had three teeth pulled so far.
So many continue to crack and break.

I'm full of bigger cavities than the ones in my teeth,
but I'd like to at least have a nice smile,
without having to lose all the money,
that I have to offer up to everything else to survive.
I've been raised in poverty.
This is the *cockroach feeling*.
Arms extend from paycheck to paycheck,
from empty pantries to empty fridges.

Isn't it hilarious how the poorer you are,
the more you have to pay?

Thoughts That Give Me the Creeps
and Notes Saved in My Phone on Impulse

1. I don't remember many interactions with my grandmother on my mother's side. I mostly only remember her funeral and watching everyone cry. I was maybe eight years old. I remember feeling bad I didn't have to fight back tears. I felt so bad I pretended to cry. That felt even worse.

2. My coworker brought up how he hadn't played a board game in so long. He said the last one he played was Life with his ex. Apparently, she was in an awful mood. He said, **"It was just a really long boring game and it wasn't that fun."** I told him, **"That sounds like the entirety of my last relationship."**

3. **"Whatever it takes to get you off."** A response that is always on repeat in my head whenever I'm in conversation or when someone asks me to do something. I feel like everyone is in a long-overdrawn foreplay session just trying to orgasm. How could they not be? What's the point if you don't?

4. Four cups of coffee and I'm ready to face anxiety. I'm ready to be dehydrated and caffeinated. I'm ready to feel like shit just enough to be awake.

5. Why is it that I can be perfectly fine day to day with not telling someone I love them until I'm fucked up on a substance? Until I'm fucked up enough to be feeling guilty because I haven't told them. I had to be on acid to feel guilty enough to talk to my closest friends. What the fuck.

6. Every day is a chess game against myself. A chess game where the winner feels twice as bad about winning and the loser gets to throw the pieces.

7. I'm staring into a space that doesn't exist. I'm thinking about your hand on my leg as the last sign of genuine affection I've received in a long time. Like years. I'm thinking about you asking me if I'm okay, and every time anyone ever asked me that haunted both my ears. I am. At least I'm trying to be.

8. Conversation Chameleon. A made-up title I gave myself one day. Behold the Conversation Chameleon, he who is the wearer of many masks. That whole day was spent mirroring other people's energy. Yes, you are excited I am excited. Yes, you are upset about that thing, I am upset about that thing. I felt so awful when I got home. This has been ongoing. I've felt so fucking awful.

9. **"Are you feeling like an ambulance? You keep rescuing everyone."** This was repeating in my head. Over and over. I need to stop trying to give everyone advice. I need to stop trying to save everyone by offering chunks of myself as collateral. Holy shit, I really do.

10. These beers will help me sleep better than you ever did. Any available depressants I can get my hands on will be better than you were.

11. My migraines are just my other selves settling in. The lights signal the arrival and my body is shared. The nausea and unease are something I'll have to get used to.

12. You need to learn when to say you're sorry even if it's apologizing to something that hurt you too.

13. There's a scene in the movie 'Crazy, Stupid, Love' where Steve Carell is told by his wife that she cheated on him. I'm pretty sure it's the first scene. Steve Carell's character is quiet as he is being bombarded all the details by his wife.

She's rambling. At one point he's had enough, and he unbuckled his seat belt, opened the door and goes limp to fall out of the moving car. I think I would jump out of a car too. It's the only proper response.

14. **"If you have any bad ideas let me know. I'm starting a collection."** I kept picturing someone asking me this. Like they were asking me for a handful of bad ideas. A smirk on their face because they really knew me. Because they knew I was full of them. Because they truly knew me. That's terrifying.

15. Compared to you, death by fire doesn't seem so bad.

16. If I ignore temptation is it growth, or am I censoring myself? Am I getting better or worse?

17. Make amends. Stop being so prideful. You said some awful shit. What if you die today? Fucking idiot.

18. It's rare that I feel in the moment. I'm always trying to figure out if anyone ever is in the moment or if we are all pretending. I want to be so taken by something that I am completely there. Not wandering off somewhere else.

19. I think about this one argument with my last ex more than anything about our relationship. Not any of the good or bad. Just the argument. It was about disinfectant and how it literally can't kill 100% of germs. She thought it was made like that so it wouldn't kill any good germs. I think about it all the time and laugh. Isn't that hilarious or maybe I'm just an asshole? Or both!

20. I'm at a point of exhaustion. My body on the verge of melting. Stagnancy, I'm trying to say farewell.

So Many Hands Have a Hold on Me

I'm spread apart,
existing in so many places at once.

1993 in a hospital,
in the hands of my mother,
for a moment.
2003 in a midwestern home,
next to a farm,
in the hands of evil.
2014 in the sunshine,
in the water,
in the heat,
in the hands of someone who loved me.

And it's easy to be this way,
this way,
when it's all you've known.

I'm finding all the fuses,
and setting them on fire,
following them back to myself.
When the dynamite I've hidden finally goes off,
won't that be something?
When everything I know explodes.

I Guess If You're Going to Bite My Face Bite Hard

Do you think,
that if we loved each other enough,
we'd look like two wild animals,
trying to eat each other,
when we fucked?

Or would that have to be hate?
Hateful glue.
Hate filled moans.
Hate so strong,
that nothing could pull us apart?

In the Voice of Sam Elliot

"**Now you look like a man who's had a night's worth of whiskey to think about all his problems.**"
The man mumbled as his gaze moved from your left hand back to your face. The bags under your eyes twitch as you grit your teeth.
"**And judging by that pistol in your hand, I'd reckon you came up with an answer to 'em.**"
Feeling restless and groggy you start to walk towards the door only to stumble into the table knocking over the glasses of water. Shattering and splashing you.
"**You know, you've got no business singing these blues looking that green, son. That's green enough to kill a man because he's got something you don't.**"
That's exactly what you intend to do. Kill a man because he's got something you don't.

How'd You Get That Scar? Hostility?

I hate the way my lips cave in,
like they're asking for approval.

Some days I want to take a knife,
and make everyone else's mouth match mine.
Chapped, scarred and angry.

Well those days I never have one handy.

Nothing Happens for a Reason

When I was seven years old,
another boy tried to bite my finger off.
Everyone gives me the same look when I tell them this.
A face of surprise and pity mixed together.

This was unprovoked.
I found out later that most awful things that happen to you,
are unprovoked.

I don't think there was any specific reason,
that he got it in his mind to gnaw on me.
He didn't think I'd look better,
with four fingers on my left hand.
He didn't want to taste my blood.
Something just snapped.

There was no reason at all.
He was just angry.
He just wanted to bite me.

There was no reason at all.

Emergency Exits

You can pretend every building is on fire,
when you run through the emergency exit.

I've been haunted every day by plenty of things,
former lovers, my cats, bad decisions,
and my need for anyone who will lend an ear to listen.

They're all fuel to the fire that only burns me.

So if you see me running,
you should know that I've had enough.
Pulling the fire alarm was just for fun.
It's all been just for fun I promise,
just for fun.

I'm nothing if not a demand for attention.

Does it Hurt? Being Touched?

Unexplainable absence,
or maybe I just don't know what to do with myself.
Day to day empty,
where you'd do anything just to feel something.

You don't hate your life,
you're just bored.
Everything surrenders to your apathy.

You're feeling like you're falling,
down and behind.
Like you've had enough and you're trying to eat yourself.
Death by digestion.
Licking the plate clean as you fall to the floor,
down and behind.
You're always feeling down and behind.

Your body's not meant to last,
you always have trouble keeping this in mind.
Especially when you're shoveling so much terrible in,
just to feel something easy,
to feel something kind.
But like the people you touch,
it isn't enough,
and none of these substances will suffice.

You can't rent intimacy,
like you've been trying to,
with all those nasty things you do.

If escape was that easy,
we'd all do it.

Hail to The King of Soothing

Seems like,
all I'm good at is seeping,
into someone's weakness,
and molding its shape.
They've asked me to become a part of them.

Never needed otherwise.
Never needed.

I'm the store bought serotonin,
the distraction.
The quick drying glue,
you've decided to use,
on all your problems.

Hail to the King of Soothing,
the King of Discount Therapy,
the King of Giving Out All His Energy,
the King of Only Being Wanted Half the Time.

His kingdom of Always Available.

Paranoia

Paranoia that the humanoid creature laying on my floor during sleep paralysis is real. That it could touch me.
Paranoia that I don't really have sleep paralysis. That the body I see hides underneath the bed when I am able to move around the room. Only appearing when I am defenseless.
Paranoia that it is able to quickly crawl to new hiding places every time I would see it.
A shuffling sound would be heard if I knew where to listen.
Paranoia that reality bends like my neck when I sleep wrong. That reality is as fragile as my spine. Cracking whenever I've moved, sore whenever I've stood still, and aching throughout the day.
Paranoia that everything currently existing or that has existed only manifests itself in what I am intermittently shown or exposed to. Paranoia that if I can be in such a state to perceive or hallucinate, I could create something worse. Something that could touch me. What other reality could manifest?
What else could be hiding on my floor?

Suicidal Pumpkin Seeds

Some of my closest friends have told me they frequently
think about suicide.
I remember once being told while I was really drunk.
While they were crying a lot.
I'm usually told everything while I'm drunk,
or drink in hand on my way there.
Usually someone isn't crying.

They were biding time.
They wanted to make enough money to get out.
Make enough money to buy a gun.
Make enough money to leave everyone behind.
I felt like I was being hollowed.
A Jack-o'-lantern,
seeds being scooped out.
Like being told this manifested a hand,
to rip out the inside.
I felt selfish because I never noticed,
and they never told me any of this before.
We stayed up all night drinking and talking.
We talked about all the fucked up things we shrugged off as
kids.
We talked about guilt.
We talked about being alive and the weight it carries.

I'm noticing more patterns every day,
between all my friends.
The habits,
the fucked up things that happen to us.
I always ask how my friends are doing,
I don't want to hear about them through someone else,
telling me how bad they got.
Telling me the worst imaginable.

The Question is If You'll Spit Me Out or Not?

Self-love is hard,
especially when you're as soft as me.
Mouthful of Jell-O pudding.
I don't know who I'm kidding.
Your teeth are going to bite through me so easily.

That's okay.
It's a good thing I'm so soft all around.
I wouldn't want to crack your tooth when you bite down.

Forest Full of Mint

I am not grand. I aspire to be, however, as much as possible.
My body flooded with the desire to be more.
Weeds sprout from my head whenever thoughts take root,
blooming ideas that break through the skull.
I am the forest full of mint and potential.
The weakness of being human is to see the ability to take
action and choose not to, through lack of discipline or
struggle to do nothing. I have made choices that started fires.
I have made choices to manifest the quicksand,
to stand still and be swallowed.

Stagnancy,
a cousin to quicksand considers itself my friend.
Considers its place in my life without asking first.
Often does it aim to grab my ankles or tie my shoelaces
together.
Desperate to make me the company it keeps.
But as stagnancy has its hands on me,
I've found myself reaching for it.
A habit I am trying to kill.

I have never been grand nor do I want to be.
But I seek to become as much as possible.
To puncture the bone and bloom.
To be the weed that refuses to be killed with pesticides,
or by standing still.

Yeah You Might Want to Get A Napkin

I might put my life on a drunken parade,
but that doesn't mean I'm asking for your opinion.
Just try to enjoy the show.

I know you feel inclined to tell me how I'm fucking up.

My throats starting to itch,
with how much anger is swelling in it.
Brow furrowed,
I'm feeling sick holding this conversation.

If I let it all go,
and threw up on you,
how fast do you think I could get out of it?

How fast do you think I could just leave?

Don't You Want To Play Today?

Devil on your shoulder,
do you want to play yet?
I could suggest some bad things,
in so many ways.
I'm really just a contained evil,
that you keep coming back too.

Leaking out my temptation,
it's making its way to your ear.
Are you anxious?
Let me help.

What a fun mess we are going to make together.

You Could Writhe With Me

If I'm on rock bottom,
I'll writhe in the dirt.
This is where I belong.
I can survive the glances,
eyes have never hurt.

If it's only looks,
I could swim in them.
I've always loved when beautiful eyes,
give me disapproving glances.

Kiss me hard next time,
there's enough room on the ground for both of us.
We'd look so beautiful.

There's plenty of room for you here with me.

Parallel Universe Me Has No Scars

Another night at the bar and I'm ordering for everyone.
Drink in hand and negative thoughts in mind,
I'm told by all of my friends I look just like the bartender.
Don't you love faces that look similar to yours?
Or does it feel like the mirror just followed you from home?

I started thinking about his life and if he enjoyed bartending. He had a look of melancholy plastered onto his face as he poured a couple shots for the party on the other side of the bar. I started wondering if we were related. Somehow the universe decided it was time for me to meet someone who shares the same blood.

"Hello! Did you happen to be abandoned also?" I would have asked given if at all that sort of thing in this reality was a little more likely. But hey, stranger things have happened. I know I've got an older brother I've never met, who's to say it's not him? Or even who's to say this isn't just another version of me?

As I sipped my whiskey and darted back and forth between conversations, I thought about the multiverses colliding with one another. Adding other versions of me into the mix. We'd probably all kill each other. I thought about how lucky some of my other alternate selves must be. Maybe some of them had their shit together. Maybe some of them didn't panic when being touched. Maybe they didn't have a body that needed to be fixed immediately after being born.

Whether the bartender is me from another reality has yet to be proven, but the fact that I think too much, especially while drinking has. Our faces had no matching scars.

No scars. Parallel universe me would have no scars.

Still Life With Misunderstanding

Maybe I gave Leigh-Cheri your likeness.
Maybe I relate too much to the woodpecker.
Tom Robbins couldn't help me solve the problem with redheads.
I thought you could.

In this vulnerable state I suppose I'm just a romantic.

I forgot how it felt to be a lover,
I looked too hard for the meaning of the moon,
and at you.
Especially at you.

I'm Doing Fantastic How Are You?

I'm wishing for a day where I don't feel obligated to ask a coworker how they're doing.
I'm wishing for a day where they don't respond with **"I'm good, how are you?"**
I'm wishing for a day where I don't have to continue the ruse with **"I'm good, thanks!"**
Holy fuck, I am suffocating in meaningless conversation.
The *cycle of good* will never end.

I'm waiting for the day,
someone tells me what's really happening in their life.

Sometimes I'll say that I'm not feeling great,
or that things have been hard,
and there is no real reason I can give them.
They never ask why or further the conversation.

It must be so uncomfortable.

I'm waiting for a day every retail store mysteriously burns to the ground and no one can give me a real reason as to why.

I Fought a Monster I Swear

Sometimes children will ask me what's wrong with my face.
Specifically my nose and lip.

Sometimes I make a funny face and say,
"It got stuck like this one day!"
Other times I make a triumphant face and say,
"I got into a fight with a monster! You should see him!"
Sometimes I'm honest and say,
"I was born this way."
They always laugh,
and I laugh too.
Their parents are usually never thrilled,
but I love how honest kids are.
One day while working,
a little girl was staring at me,
because she had a face like mine.
I smiled at her and she smiled back,
then hid behind her father.
I can still remember his face,
it was sad and wore a familiar empathy.
I feel like it's because he knew,
he knew how honest kids can be.
He knew what it would be like for his daughter,
sporting differences.
All the names she would be called,
and how her self-esteem would crumble,
any time someone asked about her face.

Every child I see with a face like mine,
born with cleft lip and palate.
I know will grow up facing the same difficulties,
that I did.

Awful Things Vending Machine

I've got a couple bucks in quarters,
for the awful things vending machine.
It's either that or the play at your own risk crane game.

At least with this I know what I'm getting.
An expected loss is more appealing,
than blindly grabbing for something,
and getting nothing.

Like exactly what I've been doing.

I've been gambling since I was a kid,
with all the games I've played,
you'd think me an expert,
someone who knows the secret to winning,
or how to have fun.
But I don't.

Intrusive Thoughts

1. The almost overpowering urge to drench the couple that were arguing about their sex life, loudly, with Raid. Jesus Christ, just buy some toys or see other people. I had no desire to hear about this at work. It was too early. The only solution was the bug spray at hand. **"Go away pests, go away."**

2. Looking down at Koi fish in a local sushi and hibachi restaurant, I wondered if there was a big enough one to swallow me whole. Lurking somewhere at the bottom barely out of view. A big enough Koi fish that could take all my consciousness in one gulp. Instead of jumping face first into the indoor pond, I settled on spending fifty cents to offer them fish pellets. They looked happy about it.

3. Feeling annoyed one night while out with friends I kept looking down at my glass of beer. Thinking if I just squeezed hard enough, I could shatter the glass in my hand. My blood on the table a good enough excuse to dismiss myself to the bathroom. A little bit of peace. Eventually making my way back to them, hand bandaged in paper towels. **"Yes, sorry about that. Please continue."** However, I just ordered more and chugged them down to try and stand being in public.

4. During work one day, there was a man with his back to me standing in front of the TV section, probably just looking to waste my time. Yes, he'd want me to tell him all about TV's and not buy any of them. For some reason all I could do was wonder how much hate I would have to stare into the back of someone's head before it burst, and confetti made its triumphant escape into the air. While I glared in his direction, my animosity growing, his wife came over and smacked him in the back of the head. In a shrill voice she exclaimed, **"We don't need another TV!"**

Parallel Universe Me Has No Scars

5. Daydreams about my skeleton coming out of my body and killing everyone around me. My skin and muscle seamlessly falling off the bone. Organs following quickly behind. My skeleton feels no anxiety. My skeleton is angry. This happens often. **"Local man's entire skeleton leaves his body and goes on a killing spree, burns down a gas station, and breaks into a Halloween store. More at eleven."**

6. The image of me talking appearing in my mind while having a conversation. A vivid real time visual of my mouth moving to what I'm saying. The way my teeth look, and lips move. This usually contributes to an increasing feeling of insecurity that lasts until the conversation is over.

7. The fear everyone is playing a game with me. The kind of pretending children do. Nothing is real. It's all one big joke and I am the punchline. I will laugh when talking to someone if I suspect the game is beginning. So, they think I don't know. Just in case.

8. How many fires could I set without being caught? How much would burn? If I am close to the fire, I want to feed it. This is literally and metaphorically accurate.

9. The idea stays in my head that we all go through the exact same thing at different times, too many coincidences happen in unison for it not to be true. I read somewhere that our entire universe is essentially just math. Big numbers. Individually we are all at different points of the equation, but ultimately, we are all part of the same equation.

10. While eating I wonder how much nutrition is there. Most food we consume has the nutritional value of a piece of cardboard. You are what you eat! Which explains why I've felt like an empty box.

A Bicycle Built For Two

You never forget how to ride a bike.
You never forget how to ride a tandem bike by yourself.
You never forget how to divide,
and then come back together,
while riding a tandem bike by yourself.

You'll never forget your entire body splitting in half,
as if it was an instinctual behavior,
to fill the empty seat of your tandem bike.

You've found yourself going through a sort of whole body
mitosis at an inconvenient time.
You were never good at math,
especially division,
but look at you now.

You and your divided other begin to hum Daisy Bell,
as you continue to cycle along unphased.
You think to yourself,
this must be a new kind of narcissism.

You'd look sweet upon the seat of a bicycle built for two.

You Stalked Me but Only in My Head

It used to be so hard to turn corners,
my eyes would play tricks on me.
Soon it was impossible for me to trust anything.

Was it justified paranoia?
If I wasn't careful,
every redhead would turn into you.

What a nightmare.

Sour Pink Lemonade

All the better things in my life have a leash on me.
Feeling trapped,
I've felt bad about a lot of things,
I shouldn't have to feel bad about wanting to be free.
Wanting to crush the fruit in my palm,
and smash everything I could reach.
I dream of pulp.

I'm trying to crack myself in two,
so you all can really get a good look.
I'm trying to let all the juice leak out.
Sour pink lemonade,
is the only proper comparison,
for my acidic insides.

My whole life has been an attempt,
and will continue to be.

Are You the Moment or The Sun?

Every step I take is my moth to your flame.
My wings feel the heat as your fire spits out my name.
I'm no stranger to consequence.
I'll fly straight into the Sun full confidence,
grinning with pompousness,
just like Icarus.

I'm going to lose if it's a battle of endurance.
My wings will give out and I'll fall into the ocean currents.

His wings were wax.
Mine are my own,
not much better.
Just mistakes and feathers,
they'll burn forever.

Do you think Icarus thought about anything in particular?
Falling into the ocean?
How close he was to the sun?
The sting of the hot wax on his skin?
Did he curse himself for his arrogance?

Or was the breeze all the way down so nice,
that all he could do was close his eyes,
and enjoy the moment?

THIS IS THE END. AND IF YOU MUST LEAVE, KISS ME GOODBYE.

Photo by @truecalidad

Matthew Stegman,

26, is the author of *If Anyone Can Hide it, it's Me*. He has been writing since he was a sophomore in high school. He has no notable accomplishments, but he makes up for it in charisma. Throughout his life Matthew has always had a passion for literature and art. The Altruistic Hedonist, The Uneducated Prick, he strives every day to be a little better than the last. Living in Florida, he continues to write and work on his many creative projects.